# TARGET AMERICA

### The Influence of Communist Propaganda on U.S. Media

## James L. Tyson

REGNERY GATEWAY
CHICAGO

Published by Regnery Gateway, Inc.
360 West Superior Street
Chicago, Illinois 60610-0890

Manufactured in the United States of America

Library of Congress Catalog Card Number: 80-54762
International Standard Book Number: 0-89526-837-X

# Contents

# Preface

Since 1950, the United States has fought two wars, both against countries vastly inferior to us militarily, economically, and in terms of population and resources. North Korea and North Vietnam were third or fourth rate countries, but against one the best we could do was fight to a draw. In Vietnam, we suffered a humiliating and costly defeat.

It was with words and ideas that our enemies frustrated our military might in Korea and Vietnam. They demonstrated the continuing validity of the old adage, "The pen is mightier than the sword." Their target was the morale of both our troops in the field and our civilian population, but especially the latter. As we embark—and rightly so—on an expensive effort to reconstitute our military might, we must recognize that the best weapons system in the world will do us no good if we continue to disregard our vulnerability on the battlefield of words.

In the years following WW II, when we were confronted with enemies affiliated with the international communist network, we neglected the power of words and ideas even though we knew that the communists were masters of propaganda and disinformation. In this vital area, we literally practiced unilateral disarmament, abandoning all defense and gutting our offensive capabilities, leaving only a hollow shell.

Despite a wealth of incontrovertible evidence to the contrary, our people are constantly bombarded with assurances that defenses against the enemy's war of words and ideas are not only unnecessary but damaging to our cause.

The longshoreman philosopher, Eric Hoffer, in his 1952 book, *Ordeal of Change,* has tried to warn us against this folly:

> We know that words cannot move mountains, but they can move the multitude; and men are more ready to fight and die for a word than for anything else. Words shape thought, stir feelings and beget actions; they kill and revive, corrupt and cure. The "men of words"—priests, prophets, intellectuals—have played a more decisive role in history than military leaders, statesmen, and businessmen.

No less important than the priests, prophets and intellectuals are those who staff and control the mass communications media. As a long-time media critic, I have been appalled to observe the ease with which important media organs in this country have been enlisted to assist in a campaign against this country, a massive and frighteningly successful war of words, inspired by governments that despise and fear freedom, aided by a host of witting and unwitting helpers.

Truth in labeling is enforced for goods on the shelves of grocery stores, but not for what you see in the newspapers or on television. Communist writers are published in such prestigious and influential papers as The *New York Times* without being properly identified. Communist propaganda is not only aired over our public broadcasting facilities, but is even financed with grants from the taxpayer-funded Corporation for Public Broadcasting. It is not, of course, so labeled.

In *Target America,* James Tyson documents the baleful record and shows us why the United States is frighteningly vulnerable. It should alert the American people to the fact that wars are fought and won with words and ideas as much as with missiles, planes, tanks and ships. And these wars go on even when we are at peace.

*Reed Irvine*

# I. Introduction

During 1980 the American people displayed several signs of growing anger and alarm at continuing Soviet aggression and American reversals abroad. In November, this concern was a major factor in the defeat of the Carter Administration and several appeasement minded senators.

But anxiety about America's position in the world continues. The trends of the past decade cannot be reversed overnight, and in recent years, many of the ablest observers of our defense situation went so far as to declare that if these trends persisted, the U.S. could be defeated by the Soviet Union within the next ten years. Brian Crozier, one of Great Britain's leading students of strategy, published a study of the peril of the West, entitled *Strategy of Survival* in 1978, in which he says the democracies face defeat in the near future. "Unless the West reacts *now,*" he concludes, "meaning by 1980, the chances are that the tide of retreat will be irreversible."

Several Americans defense experts are equally concerned but reluctant to be so frank for publication.

The closer the observer is to the facts of Soviet preparations, the more worried he is. The most worried of all are those Russian emigrés *who have seen Communist preparations from the inside.* Dr. Igor S. Glagolev was a member of the Soviet Academy of Sciences and an adviser to the Russian SALT I negotiators. After the treaty was signed, he recommended some logical armaments cuts. He was shocked to be told by his superiors that they had no intention of reducing their arms, but instead planned to increase them until they had overwhelming superiority. In disillusionment, he defected to the West in 1976, settled in Washington, and has been waging a one-man warning campaign ever since.

Another better known emigré, of course, is Alexander Solzhenitsyn, who has also been a tireless Jeremiah, warning America of probable defeat if we do not regain our courage. "Will you wait until the Communists are beating at your gates and your sons will have to defend your borders with their breasts?" he cried in one of his most dramatic appeals.

The Soviets are following a three-part strategy: (1) the enormous arms buildup, as Glagolev warns, hidden under the smoke screen of detente and the SALT negotiations; (2) a gradual take-over of other weaker countries by pro-Communist regimes, leading to the eventual encirclement of the U.S. on the outside; and (3) a massive, secret propaganda campaign designed to weaken and demoralize America from the inside.

The first two threats are recognized by some of the public and many of our leaders. But the third is virtually unknown except to a few specialists. And it may be as dangerous as the first two because of the fact that the public is not even aware of it.

This propaganda campaign has been going on with increasing vigor and long-range planning ever since the Bolshevik Revolution. It is designed to undermine our confidence in our own democratic system and our leaders, to destroy our trust in our security agencies (the FBI, CIA, and police forces) so that the Communists can operate more freely against us in this country and abroad, and to undermine our foreign policy so that we fail to support our allies in the fight against Communism and allow the encirclement to continue almost unopposed.

If this forecast of encirclement sounds alarmist, just consider the history of the past 40 years. In 1939, there was only one Communist country, the Soviet Union, accounting for about 7% of the earth's population. In 1940, the Soviets swallowed up the three Baltic Republics. In succeeding years, we have seen the communization of all Eastern Europe, Czechoslovakia, North Korea, China, North Viet Nam, Cuba, South Viet Nam, Cambodia, Laos, Mozambique, Angola, South Yemen, Ethiopia, Nicaragua, Grenada, Surinam, and Afghanistan. As a result, Communist governments now control more than a third of the world's population. The Communists prepared for every one of these conquests by a massive campaign of propaganda and subversion before taking any military action. For all of Eastern Europe, China, Cuba, South Viet Nam, Cambodia, and Angola, they also waged clever propaganda campaigns in the U.S. and Western Europe to confuse the democracies and undermine our resolve to resist this Communist imperialism.

While the American people are waking up to the

Communist political and military threat, it is time they were awakened to this propaganda threat. Only if we become aware of it can we neutralize it. In its present largely undercover form, it represents one of the most serious dangers facing the country today.

How is it possible to illustrate the effects of such Communist propaganda in the United States? It has become difficult in recent years to identify Communists agents in the media or other influential organizations. The FBI has been ordered not to investigate subversive activity unless there is *already evidence of criminal behavior.* This restriction has literally wrecked the Bureau's ability to monitor Communist subversion. (How can you get evidence of criminal behavior until you have first conducted an investigation?) The FBI's number of open cases of security investigations dropped from 21,414 in 1973 to 50 in 1979. This was made clear in an exchange of correspondence between the Bureau and Senator Gordon Humphrey of the Senate Armed Services Committee in late 1979. Several senators on this Committee were concerned that the Soviets were attempting to manipulate American media and public opinion to obtain a SALT II Treaty favorable to the USSR.

On August 22, 1979, Humphrey wrote William Webster, director of the FBI, recommending a study of Communist propaganda in the U.S. as being of benefit to several matters of Armed Services Committee concern. Humphrey received a letter from Webster on November 19, saying, "This Bureau does not have a data base upon which to predicate a study or discussion of such issues, since we do not dedicate personnel to tracking the sources of news articles bearing on

U.S.-USSR relations to see if they were Soviet in-spired. . . . In view of the foregoing, the unclassified study requested in your letter of August 22 cannot be undertaken. . . ."

Not only the FBI's counter-subversion efforts, but the congressional committees that used to investigate Communist (as well as right-wing) subversion, have all been dismantled, including the Senate Internal Securities Subcommittee, the Senate Subcommittee on Criminal Laws and Procedures, and the House Internal Security Committee. The Subversive Activities Control Board has also been abolished, all under the theory that the Cold War is an outdated concept. As a result, the only media personalities who can be positively identified as present or former Communists today are those of *the older generation,* whose careers extend back into the years when there were active investigations of subversives.

But there are two techniques we can use to provide at least strong circumstantial evidence of Communist influence:

## The "Balance Sheet" method:

Draw up a balance sheet listing all the major stories, articles, or broadcasts of the media personality in question. These can be listed under two major headings: (a) debits—those that appear to follow the current Communist line, or (b) credits—those written from a position harmful to the Communist line. It may be that many of the articles under (a) are based some-what on true facts. The Communists frequently select their propaganda campaigns in areas where there is a large element of truth (for example, corruption or lack of ideal democracy in a small country under attack by Communists—as we shall see below for Cambodia). But if the writer in question shows a balance sheet with all his articles on the debit—pro-Communist—side, and *none* on the credit side, this may not be firm proof that he is an agent, but it is certainly strong evidence that he is being useful to the USSR. Six such balance sheets are presented in Chapter X for four individuals and two think tanks, whose activities are described more fully in other chapters.

## The Case History method:

Prepare a brief case history of media treatment of a major subject whose treatment can now be shown to have been based so clearly on *false information* and at the same to have *followed the Communist line so closely* that it must have been the work either of agents or of Communist manipulation. Later chapters employ this technique. They present seven case histories illustrating how major issues in American foreign or defense policies were the subject of Communist propaganda that can now be shown to have been based on *falsehoods*. These chapters will also describe how such campaigns affected public opinion, and in some cases, government policy as well.

The United States and most of the Soviet Union's other major targets are democracies. The distinguishing feature of democracies is that they believe themselves to be ruled by their own public opinion. When the Soviet Union succeeds in planting clandestine propaganda in any democratic country, it in effect diminishes the importance of that country's genuinely domestic opinion. This is the very definition of subversion, and what the Soviet Union is well practiced at doing.

The means by which clandestine propaganda is spread are quite indistinguishable from those of covert political action and very close to those of clandestine intelligence collection. All these means involve finding persons in the target country who, for whatever reason, wittingly, semi-wittingly, or unwittingly, are willing to produce the line of argument favored by the Communists or to insure that the opposing points of view are killed. Countries affected by successful covert propaganda may suffer internal demoralization, controversy, and eventual surrender, and in the end, blame it on "divisions within our society," "selfish corporations," "big labor unions," and other groups we hear falsely blamed so often when democracies criticize themselves.

How much money does the Soviet Union spend on propaganda and how many propaganda agents have they been able to place or recruit in the United States? It is impossible to get exact figures but all estimates are so huge that they provide an astonishing picture of the size of the Soviet effort.

The CIA puts the figure for Soviet spending on propaganda around the world, outside the USSR, at more than $3 billion. Suzanne Labin, a French expert on Communism, estimated in 1967 that the Communists had more than 500,000 propaganda agents around the world, outside the USSR. These figures can be compared with even more direct sources on the number of people engaged in propaganda *within the Soviet Union. Pravda* revealed in 1970 that there were 1.1 million full time propagandists or "agit-props" within the USSR. A Soviet scholarly journal provided a total for part time and full time propagandists of 6.8 million, which includes no less than 80,000 "atheist lecturers."

The position of agit-prop is a prestigious one in the Soviet apparatus, considered to be as respectable a profession as accountancy or civil engineering in the U.S. There are no less than six professional journals for propagandists, which we could compare to the *Journal of Accountancy* or the *Engineering News Record* in the U.S. One of these, *The Agitator,* is used mainly for foreigners. Lee Harvey Oswald read it regularly during his years in the Soviet Union, and tried to subscribe, after his return to the U.S. Every political unit in the USSR, from provinces down to villages, has a party organization with at least three officials, the chairman, the secretary, *and the agit prop*.

If one considers that the Communist Party has assigned these millions of people to carry out propaganda *against their own citizens within the Soviet Union,* the estimate of a half million agents outside the country does not seem far-fetched. The various universities and schools for Communist cadres have graduated more than 120,000 people *from foreign countries* since 1926. These are the top experts, the full time professional cadres. They do not include the less fully trained: the fellow travelers and sympathizers who may have never even visited the Soviet Union.

How many of these half million agents are operating in the U.S.? Again, there are no official figures, but from several sources, it is possible to deduce that there must be a minimum of 4,000 agents, fellow travelers, or sympathizers actively supporting Communist propaganda efforts in this country. Likewise, it is possible to estimate that out of the $3 billion being spent worldwide, at least $250 million is being annually spent in the U.S. So, we have minimum estimates of more than 4,000 people, spending more than $250 million a year on a propaganda effort that most Americans do not realize even exists.

How is this broad activity organized? Again, the evidence is sketchy. Responsibility for Soviet propaganda rests not with any government department, *but with the Communist Party,* which directs a huge Department of Propaganda and Agitation responsible for both foreign and domestic efforts. This is housed in a massive building in Moscow. Alexander Kasnacheev, a KGB agent who defected to the Americans in Burma, describes occasional visits to this headquarters, where he was awed by the military discipline, elaborate security, and extreme secrecy.

The International Department, under the Politburo, is responsible for operations in non-Communist countries. This department has taken over the work formerly performed by the notorious Comintern, which in the days of operators like Grigory Zinoviev and the Hungarian, Bela Kun, was responsible for the control of Communist parties in other countries and the planning and execution of foreign propaganda and subversion. The Politburo is responsible for setting overall propaganda policies, while the International Department is in charge of carrying out these policies around the free world. Under this department is the International Information Department, responsible for such overt activities as the news services (*Tass* and *Novostii*), foreign work of *Pravda, Izvestiya,* and Radio Moscow, and the voluminous activities of Embassy Information Departments. While these operations are ostensibly public, they also include a large amount of undercover propaganda. The KGB's Department of Disinformation, another important center of power in propaganda, now known as Directorate A, is responsible for an increased level of psychological warfare around the world, consisting of the floating of forgeries, planting mendacious articles in friendly media, and similar deceptions. While other Soviet organs are responsible for more subtle propaganda, the Disinformation Directorate specializes in "outright lies," to quote Dr. Glagolev. According to Glagolev's estimate, they are now executing more than 500 such disinformation operations per year around the world. A further symptom of the Soviets' high regard for propaganda and espionage is that the KGB's Director is a member of the Politburo. (Contrast that with the U.S. where the heads of the FBI, CIA, and the International Communications Agency are well below Cabinet rank.) Another influential organ in propaganda against the United States is the Institute for the Study of the U.S.A. and Canada, a part of the Soviet Academy, headed by Dr. Georgi Arbatov.

How is the apparatus organized within the United States? Ray Wannall, former chief of the FBI's Counter-Intelligence Service, is of the opinion that since the early 1950's, Soviet propaganda against the U.S. has been directed from outside the country. Certainly, the Communist Party, U.S.A. plays only a subsidiary role. Most propaganda direction comes from the International Department of the Central Committee. In order to direct activities in the U.S., Soviet control officers travel in and out of the country. They do so under a variety of identities and pretexts. In this, the large international Communist front groups are useful. The largest of these is the World Peace Council. Other activities are transmitted through a myriad of other fronts, including the World Federation of Trade Unions (WFTU), the Women's International Democratic Federation, and the International Association of Democratic Lawyers. All of these groups maintain relations with contacts in the U.S. and promote continuous intercourse through international conferences, periodicals, and other communications. But the U.S. is so open that virtually anyone can come and go on any pretext whatever. And some of these groups have American counterparts. The World Peace Council works through the U.S. Peace Council, headed by veteran American Communist Pauline Rosen. Other links are less formal, and direct control has not been proven. But, for example, the National Lawyers Guild has close ties to the International Association of Democratic Lawyers, while Women Strike for Peace in the U.S. has a long-standing close association with the Women's International Democratic Federation. In addition, within the U.S., there has grown a large number of study centers, citizens' committees, and public affairs coalitions that maintain close relationships with these international Communist fronts. Only a few of these have been identified by congressional committees or the attorney general as Communist fronts, but all of them have one common characteristic: they consistently back causes that knowingly or unknowingly give aid or comfort to the Communists and have *never* advocated policies that are contrary to the Communist line. As a group, they can be classified under one name, "The Far Left Lobby," and will be described in the next chapter. The most important of these and their knowing or unknowing support of the Soviet propaganda organs are also summarized on Chart I on the next page.

The Chinese Communist government administers a propaganda apparatus within its own borders almost as massive as that of the Soviets. Overseas efforts are not as vast as the Soviets, but are substantial, including energetic efforts to manipulate media in other countries.

Lenin, in his writings, continually pounded on the importance of the mass media in propaganda. In 1950, Stalin said, "If I could control the movies, I could rule the world." This was before he had any concept of the power of television. In a report to the Politburo, Soviet Foreign Minister Molotov bluntly stated: "Who reads the Communist papers? Only a few people who are already Communists. We don't need to propagandize them. What is our object? Who do we have to influence? We have to influence non-Communists if we want to make them Communists or if we want to fool them. So we try to infiltrate the big press, to influence millions of people, and not merely thousands."

# ORGANIZATION OF SOVIET PROPAGANDA AND U.S. GROUPS PROVIDING KNOWING AND UNKNOWING SUPPORT

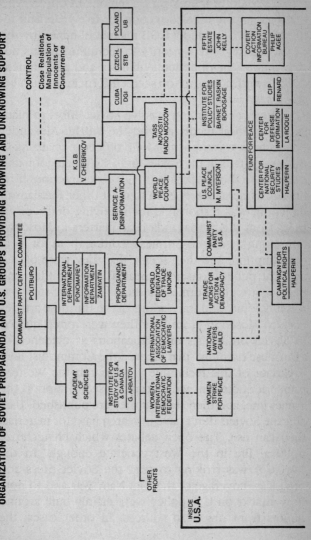

More recently, John Maury, a senior CIA officer who was head of the Russian section for five years and retired in 1977, quoted a KGB manual obtained by the CIA which gives top priority to recruiting agents not only among the opponents' military and government officials with access to top secret information, but also among *the media*.

There is a continuing massive Soviet effort to plant stories in local media around the world. Alexander Kaznecheev was the senior KGB officer specializing in Burmese affairs at the Soviet Embassy in Rangoon and defected to the Americans in 1959. He describes how his department, secret even to most other Russians in Rangoon, was responsible for receiving drafts of articles from the propaganda headquarters in Moscow, translating them into Burmese, editing them for local consumption, and then seeing that they were placed in local publications to appear as though they had been written by Burmese authors. The final step was to send copies and translations of the Burmese articles back to Moscow. From here they were often quoted in Soviet broadcasts or publications as evidence of "Burmese opinion" that favored the Communist line. A variant of this technique is to search the Western press for quotations which can be used to support the Soviet line, and then see that they are published. Usually, the Soviets don't have to search hard for materials they can use. The open debates which characterize political life in the West generate enough. In the 1970s, it was striking to read the Soviet press and broadcast coverage of the Viet Nam War and to note how attacks on U.S. policy were mainly built around quotes from American sources. In other cases, the

KGB's Disinformation Department relies on outright forgeries. American intelligence has detected innumerable cases over the years of forged documents being used to discredit American agencies or policies. Sometimes these are such obvious fakes as to boomerang on the Communists, but frequently, they leave enough smoke to lead people to believe there was some fire. A notable example was the series of Communist forgeries making it appear that the CIA had been behind the efforts by French Generals to overthrow or assassinate President De Gaulle.

Since the death of Stalin and the launching of "detente," Soviet propagandists have not abandoned old methods, but added new ones. In *The White House Years,* Henry Kissinger says that Dr. Georgi Arbatov, Director of the Institute for the Study of the U.S.A. and Canada, "knew much about America and was skillful in adjusting his arguments to the prevailing fashion. He was especially subtle in playing to the inexhaustible masochism of American intellectuals, who took it as an article of faith that every difficulty in U.S.-Soviet relations had to be caused by American stupidity or intransigence." Arbartov is regularly welcomed by academic and think-tank scholars in the U.S. and often quoted by CBS, Newsweek, the New York Times, and other media without comment as to his true motives. For example, in 1977, Dr. J. Kenneth Galbraith was the narrator of a Public Broadcasting System TV series on Socialism and Free Enterprise entitled "The Age of Uncertainty." Georgi Arbatov appeared at a luncheon table seated between Galbraith and Mrs. Katherine Graham, owner of the Washington Post-Newsweek enterprise. Late in the program, the camera focused on Arbatov, who delivered the following statement: "The Russian people love freedom!" Neither Galbraith, Graham, nor PBS pointed out to the audience that while the Russian people may indeed love freedom, Arbatov and his bosses are its enemies.

With people like Arbatov enjoying such prestigious platforms, such respectable company, and such lack of contradiction, older forms of propaganda like Radio Moscow and Russian foreign language magazines have become less significant. Our own media do a better job.

Thus in recent years, the Soviets have relied most heavily on propaganda from within—i.e., propaganda executed by citizens of the target countries themselves, by media personnel, members of public affairs organizations or front groups, and other opinion leaders who have been recruited as "agents of influence" or are being manipulated without their knowledge. In principle, propaganda from within is the most difficult and least reliable form of the art. To do it successfully, one has to stimulate great numbers of people to follow a line simply by giving them cues to which they have accustomed themselves to respond. It is difficult. But when it works, large scale propaganda campaigns can be waged without the target people even being aware that propaganda is taking place or that the Communists are behind it.

Since it is far more effective to have one's own line of propaganda written or spoken by people of the same nationality as the target population, the art of propaganda depends on inducing persons in the target populations, to, in effect, act as agents. Some of the best propaganda assets are those who genuinely believe they have a mind of their own, yet follow their cues almost invariably. Also, it is quite normal for people to associate themselves with a propaganda effort through a front organization. Thus, their association with the effort, effective as it might be at any given time, is only secured by tenuous bonds.

The modern techniques of propaganda from within requires not so much manipulated front groups as congenial groups encouraged to do their own thing. According to Miles Copeland, a retired CIA officer, the CIA dubbed this technique the "Franchise System" and compared it to the way franchises operate in the field of fast food. The Communists have been encouraging every radical organization around the world that was pushing anything approaching the Communist line or *any line opposed to the United States*. They scaled down their efforts to *control* every such organization, first because it was becoming impossible, and second, because it was unnecessary.

Encouragement might take the form of money or advice for smaller organizations (often without such organizations knowing the source), or even manpower and weapons for larger groups.

The Soviets regularly go so far as to give secret support to Trotskyite or Maoist groups that are ostensibly opposed to the Soviet Union or supporting Communist China. The only criterion is that they be opposed to the United States on the principle that any enemy of my enemy is my friend. "Let's go after the U.S. now," General Agayants, first Director of the KGB's Disinformation Department, was quoted as saying. "We can take care of China later." The U.S. is "glavny vrag," the main enemy.

Up until 1968, the Soviets had given only lukewarm

support to many of the New Left groups, believing them too crazy, irrational, and hard to control. But after 1968, when they saw that the New Left played a major role in the retirement of Lyndon Johnson and the near downfall of Charles De Gaulle and had put a major crimp in the U.S. Viet Nam effort, they began to take them more seriously and support them actively, even though many such groups were unaware of the support and in some cases continued to attack the Soviet Union.

The recently retired head of the Counter-Intelligence Division of the FBI, Ray Wannall, says that the Communists in recent years are doing more of their recruiting of Americans in foreign countries during international conferences, foreign visits, and other occasions. A typical instance is the Venceremos Brigade. From 1968 onwards, Cuban and North Vietnamese intelligence agents in the U.S. were active in persuading young radical activists in the U.S. to join this Brigade, which ostensibly was helping with sugar harvests, teaching school, and conducting other peaceful pursuits in Cuba. Many of these young people came from the Weather Underground, an extreme off-shoot of the radical Students for a Democratic Society (SDS). In fact, the Brigade became a pool for the Communists to recruit agents for work in the United States. War protest movements needed not just intellectual protesters but also physically rugged recruits for more violent duty. Such people were trained in guerilla warfare techniques, including the use of arms and explosives. One of the results was the so-called "Days of Rage" in Chicago in 1969 in which several police were injured and at least one permanently crippled. Another objective of the Cuban intelligence effort through the Brigade was the recruitment of "individuals who are politically oriented and who someday may obtain a position in the U.S. government, which would provide Cuba with access to political, economic or military intelligence."

Journalists, scholars, scientists and other visitors to Russia are also targets of recruiting efforts.

Yuri Krotkov, a Russian playwright and part-time employee of the KGB on propaganda, who defected to the West in 1965, testified before the Senate Subcommittee on Internal Security. He described how the KGB was carrying out constant efforts to subvert foreign journalists in Moscow. He cited the KGB's energetic but unsuccessful efforts to subvert two *New York Times* correspondents, Bill Jordan and Jack Raymond. But he says the Soviets were successful in recruiting the Australian journalist, Wilfred Burchett, who carried out an assignment for Ho Chi Minh to work with the Pathet Lao communists in Laos. He has also been reported by other sources to have been active in North Korea during the Korean War, attempting to propagandize American prisoners and assisting in interrogation.

Joseph Frolik, a member of the Czech intelligence service for 16 years, defected to the U.S. in 1975. In November, 1975, he testified before the Senate Subcommittee that Czech intelligence in the U.S. was closely controlled by the KGB, and was carrying out an energetic campaign to recruit among staffs of the U.S. Congress, Government departments, the Republican and Democratic parties, and "mass organizations" like the AFL-CIO, NAACP, and the American

Civil Liberties Union. During his tenure in Washington, he said, the Czech embassy attempted to penetrate Ralph Nader's organization, cooperating with Syrian intelligence to gather data on Nader's relatives in Lebannon. He had no knowledge that Nader was recruited but mentioned this as typical of Communist efforts to influence opinion leaders.

Idealism is one of the most common appeals to recruit Communist agents, fellow travelers and sympathizers. Hollywood screenwriter Dalton Trumbo claims that all the "finest people" in Hollywood joined the party in protest against Depression conditions in the 1930's. Many Hollywood Communists deserted the party after the Hitler-Stalin pact, but Trumbo and others hardlined it and remained members. They included the "Hollywood Ten", who refused to testify before the House Un-American Activities Committee in 1947, went to jail for contempt and were blacklisted by the industry. Regardless of the blacklisting, many of the Hollywood Ten succeeded in influencing the contents of movies towards a Communist line. Trumbo has boasted that they may not have managed to get pro-Communist films produced by Hollywood but they did succeed in preventing several outstanding anti-Communist stories from becoming motion pictures, most notably Arthur Koestler's great novel of the Communist purge trial period, *Darkness At Noon.*

Ambition is frequently used as an appeal. In *Beyond Cloak and Dagger: Inside the CIA,* retired senior CIA official Miles Copeland describes a type of American journalist whom the Russians call "maggots." These are reporters who have no strong opinions of their own but believe that in the current climate of opinion they can be most successful by following the anti-anti-Communist line.

Copeland says that the Soviets also identify another type they call "termites." These are individuals who are not agents but are so leftist in sympathy that they become anti-anti-Communists. Opposed to efforts to contain Communism, which they believe violate their liberal principles, they aid Communists in passing along their propaganda line.

Money is a major appeal, but sex, as a means for recruiting Americans is rated rather low by the KGB.

Alcohol is a classic persuader, used more in manipulation than in outright recruiting. Yuri Besmenoff, a recent defector from *Novostii,* the Russian News agency, now living in Canada, testified that during his apprenticeship in Moscow, one of his principle duties was to work on foreign visiting delegations. "As soon as any group got off the plane," he says, "my job was to get them drunk as soon as possible and keep them that way throughout their visit. If I had too much alcohol myself, there were always other comrades to take over from me—but there was no one to replace our delighted guests... Our first function was to make every foreigner think everything in Russia was just splendid." He adds that he personally "did such a job" on a *Look* photographer in 1967, accompanying him around Russia. He was so successful in maneuvering this American into presenting a favorable picture story of Russia that he was later rewarded with a ticket for a week in Italy.

"If foreign guests showed strong sympathy for the Soviet Union," Besmenoff says, "our job was to prepare them psychologically, and then pass them over to the KGB agents to indoctrinate and recruit them. . . The KGB trains them to destroy anti-Soviet activists in their own countries through character as-sassination and infiltrate universities, trade unions and organizations such as the Canadian-Soviet Friendship Society."

Manipulation of well-meaning persons without their knowledge is an important technique, but there are even more subtle forms of manipulation used con-stantly by the Soviet propaganda organizations. West-ern correspondents and media commentators are targets of continuous efforts. During the Eisenhower-Khrushchev Summit Conference in Geneva, in 1955, the Soviets skillfully manuvered the crowd of free world journalists into creating an exaggerated atmo-sphere of hopefulness at the start. When the confer-ence fizzled out with no real progress, the journalists were encouraged to lay much of the blame on Dulles and other democratic statesmen. The Soviet propa-ganda organs were then able to make it appear that all criticism of Western statesmen was coming from free world sources and the Westerners alone were respon-sible for the failure of the conference.

There may be little concrete evidence on the exact dimensions of the Soviet covert propaganda effort in the U.S.—with our investigative agencies crippled, how could there be?—but there are many indications that the USSR is conducting a massive, deliberate, highly effective campaign which has had a major im-pact on our national policy. In recent years, most of the implementation has been carried out *by agents and sympathizers within the U.S., mainly Americans,* working in think tanks, citizens' committees and foundations, helped by friends in media and the government. These people are primarily responsible for converting the Kremlin's basic goals into specific propaganda campaigns and devising tactics and slogans that will have the most effect on American media, public opinions and government policy.

A large number of such think tanks, citizens committees, and other organizations have grown up in recent years. Only a few of these have been identified as Communist fronts by the Attorney General or Congressional Committees, but this "Far Left Lobby," which consistently backs causes that help the Communists and *never* advocates policies that contradict the Communist line, will be discussed in detail in the next chapter.

# II.  The Far Left Lobby

*Q. "Don't you think that some people in the U.S. are always seeing Communists under the bed?"*

*Eldridge Cleaver: "But there are Communists under the bed!"*

*From* Rolling Stone *magazine, September 4, 1976, interview with the former Black Panther leader after his return from being a fugitive in several Communist countries and France.*

According to principles developed by Lenin and his associates, front groups are among the finest vehicles for Communist propaganda. The principle of fronts is to use an attraction to induce non-Communists to co-operate with Communists or to serve the Communists' objectives. As for propaganda, fronts are useful because they can spew the Communist line, yet give the impression, sometimes true, that the line is coming from non-Communist sources. Fronts can conduct research studies, seminars, publish books and pamphlets, write letters, encourage demonstrations, take legal action, and in other ways exert influence on the media. Francis Watson, an expert on subversion and terrorism, quotes a figure of no less than 2400 "movement" organizations in the U.S. The following "movement" groups, Legal Organizations, Foundations, Think Tanks, Citizens Committees, and Innocents, wield the greatest influence on the media and public policy and also show the clearest signs of following a pro-Communist line, knowingly or unknowingly. Some have been identified as Communist fronts, and many others have Communists sprinkled among their memberships.

LEGAL ORGANIZATIONS—The Communists have made a major effort to infiltrate the U.S. legal professions, for in no other country is the Law more influential in politics and even in foreign relations.

*The National Lawyers Guild.* The NLG grew out of the International Red Aid, founded by the Communist International in 1922. In 1925, this IRA set up an American Section, which in 1936, helped to organize the National Lawyers Guild, which became affiliated with the International Association of Democratic Lawyers, the world-wide Communist front. The NLG now has several thousand members and units in most leading law schools, and a major operation in Washington. When the League testifies before Congress, its views are accepted as those of strong civil libertarians. Major media often gives NLG members a sounding board, without identifying their far left tendencies. For example, at the height of the 1978 controversy over the indictment of several FBI agents for their investigation of the Weather Underground terrorists, the *New York Times* ran an Op Ed page article by Gerald Lefcourt (only identified as an attorney) attacking the FBI. Lefcourt is a leading member of the Guild and was a lawyer (in the '60s and '70s) for the Weather Underground.

Cited many times by HUAC and the Senate Internal Security Committee as a Communist front, the Guild moved for a dismissal of the listing on the grounds of "lack of prosecution." Leading officers and members include:

—David Rudocsky, also member of the NECLC, active in several suits against the CIA, FBI, and Selective Service.

—Victor Rabinowitz, member of Rabinowitz, Boudin and Standard, which has represented Alger Hiss, Communist Cuba, Daniel Ellsberg and Soviet spy Judith Coplon.

—Bernadine Dohrn, National Student Organizer, 1967-68; until recently a fugitive from justice as a Weather Underground member.

—Robert Borosage, now Director of the Institute for Policy Studies.

—William Kunstler

—Bella Abzug

—Arthur Kinroy, law partner of Kunstler's. Counsel for atom spy, Martin Sobell, the Southern Conference Education Fund (a Communist front) and the Chicago Seven.

The NLG is one of the most influential groups in the Far Left Lobby and has spawned a number of other organizations, including the following:

*The National Emergency Civil Liberties Committee,* (NECLC), founded in 1951 by NLG members, was cited as a Communist front by HUAC in 1958, for repeatedly defending Communists in legal proceedings and disseminating Communist propaganda. Clients include the "Teheran Ten," Ramsey Clark and Alger Hiss. Members include: Leonard Boudin, representative of the Cuban government and father of Weather Underground leader Kathy Boudin, now on trial in the Brink's robbery case, Sidney Gluck, Harvey O'Connor, Frank Wilkinson (identified before Congressional committees as Communist Party members), and Morton Stavis, who has taken the Fifth Amendment when asked if he was a member of the Communist Party. *The Center For Constitutional Rights,* founded in 1966 by NLG members William Kunstler, Arthur Kinroy and Morton Stavis. Its far left activities, include an attempt in the 1970s to have U.S. support of the Cambodian Government, which was fighting the bloody Pol Pot Communist guerillas, declared unconstitutional.

*The Campaign To Stop Government Spying,* renamed the *Campaign for Political Rights,* a leader in the campaign against the CIA, FBI and local law enforcement agencies, includes many radicals other than lawyers, and has drawn in more than 80 far left or well-meaning liberal organizations. Members include: Morton Halperin (Chairperson) and Frank Donner, identified as a Communist before Congressional committees.

FOUNDATIONS—the following foundations have been notable for sponsoring causes which have resulted in support for the Communist line.

*The Rubin Foundation,* one of the principal backers of the *Institute for Policy Studies* (IPS), the most important of the far left think tanks. It once gave financial support to *Breira,* a New York City Jewish organization opposed to the state of Israel, which ceased operations in 1980, probably because of the criticism of its peculiar point of view.

*The Stern Fund* has also backed the IPS and other far left groups. Its President is Philip M. Stern. Black politician Channing Phillips has said, "You are most likely to get to Philip Stern if you are doing something that threatens the system."

*The Fund For Peace,* founded by leftists and liberals, was initially backed by Stewart Mott, the largest individual shareholder of General Motors, and a supporter of leftist causes.

Other foundations which regularly back leftist projects include the *Southern Conference Education Fund* (at one time, the Communist Party's major front in the South), and the *Youth Project,* once headed by Marge Tabankin, elected to the ruling council of the Soviet-created World Peace Assembly in 1972. From time to time, many large, well-known organizations, such as the *Ford Foundation* and the *Marshall Field Foundation,* have been persuaded to finance projects which follow the Communist line.

THINK TANKS—The leading edge of the Far Left Lobby in influencing the media and public policy, the think tanks are active in sponsoring conferences and seminars, brief Congress and the executive departments, and take activist roles in law suits and mass demonstrations.

*The Institute For Policy Studies* (IPS), the most important think tank (annual budget of more than $1 million), is the center of a large web of project groups and related industries, which have consistently followed a far left line, such as unilateral disarmament for the U.S., withdrawal of support for American allies abroad, attacks on free enterprise and democratic institutions at home. (See Chapter X.) Leading personalities include Robert L. Borosage, director, former head of the NLG Washington office, Richard Barnet, Marcus Raskin, and Roberta Salper, a member of the Central Committee of the Puerto Rican Socialist Party, a pro-Communist group.

*IPS Projects and Subsidiaries:*

*National Priorities Project* (NPP) publicizes the theme that the U.S. military power is a major threat to world peace and proposes the transfer of U.S. defense funds to "more productive social goals."

*Government Accountability Project* (GAP), encourages present or former members of U.S. intelligence or other government employees to "blow the whistle" on projects they oppose.

*Bay Area Institute* (BAI), IPS San Francisco affiliate, sponsors Pacific News Service and other Coast leftist causes.

*Transnational Institute* (TNI), the major IPS vehicle for affecting international politics. Former director, Orlando Letelier, who had been foreign minister of Chile under Salvador Allende's pro-Communist government, was killed in Washington by a bomb planted in his car, in November, 1976. His briefcase was recovered intact from the wreckage. It contained correspondence and records that provided an inside look at how IPS and its related groups fit into the pro-Communist propaganda network. Among other things, the letters showed that Letelier had received a lump sum of $5,000 and was receiving $1,000 monthly from Beatrice Allende in Havana, the daughter of Salvador Allende, and the wife of the number two man in the Cuban intelligence service.

This and other evidence in the correspondence proved that Letelier was in the pay of an international propaganda network, based in East Berlin and administered by Cuban and Chilean Communists, but ultimately controlled and mainly financed by the Soviet KGB. There is a clear indication that Letelier and the IPS were not working for true democracy in Chile or elsewhere, but rather for their own brand of Socialism. In a letter to Beatrice Allende, Letelier says that he is doing everything possible to oppose the movement to back Eduardo Frei, a popular leader and true democrat, in Chile as a possible alternative to the Junta. In the same letter, Letelier says, "Perhaps some day, not far away, we will be able to do what has been done in Cuba." In other words, he and the IPS were working for a Cuban-styled Communist dictatorship in Chile, not for democracy.

*The Fund For Peace Constellation,* next to IPS the three most important far left think tanks, are grouped around the *Fund for Peace:*

*The Center for International Policy* (CIP), working through a network of journalists, former diplomats and international officials world-wide, most CIP publications consistently attack U.S. aid to "repressive" regimes of countries cooperating with the U.S. in opposing Communists. CIP director William Goodfellow, an apologist for the Pol Pot regime in Cambodia, in a *New York Times* Op Ed article said that the reports of massacres in that country were false and the results of "self-serving propaganda."

*The Center for Defense Information* (CDI), promotes through publications, speeches, conferences, unilateral U.S. disarmament, minimizing Soviet build-up.

*The Center for National Security Studies* (CNSS), is the leading critic of the CIA, FBI and other intelligence law enforcement activities. (See Chapter X.)

*The North American Congress on Latin America* (NACLA), has considerable influence in media treatment of CIA and American Policy in Latin America.

CITIZENS COMMITTEES—Back positions coinciding with the Communist line and never advocate opposing positions.

*Committee for Public Justice,* formed by Lillian Hellman, an admitted former Communist, and Ramsey Clark, monitors the FBI, CIA and Justice Department, advocates policies weakening these groups.

*The Indochina Resource Center,* (now the *Southeast Asia Resource Center*) consistently backed the North Vietnamese and Cambodian Communists and has continued to defend them in recent years in spite of the growing evidence of their brutality.

*Campaign for Economic Democracy,* founded by Tom Hayden and his actress turned activist wife, Jane Fonda.

*Organizing Committee for a Fifth Estate,* original publishers of *Counter Spy* magazine, which spawned *Covert Action Information Bulletin,* publications which identified and mis-identified undercover American personnel. The murder of the CIA's Athens station chief and shots fired at the home of the CIA's Kingston, Jamaica station chief followed publication of their identities.

*Riverside Church Disarmament Program,* organized by the Church's senior minister, the Rev. William Sloane Coffin, as a major activity of the Church, under the directorship of Cora Weiss (daughter of the founder of the Rubin foundation). Ms. Weiss had been prominent in groups opposing U.S. support for Viet Nam, as was Rev. Coffin, one of the founders of Clergy and Laity Concerned, a group opposed to the U.S. Policy in View Nam, which continues to back causes paralleling the Communist line. Under Coffin and Weiss, the Riverside program has actively promoted unilateral U.S. disarmament.

*Women Strike for Peace,* in the forefront of agitation against a resumption of testing by the U.S. and conspicuously silent in protesting Soviet violations. Has continued to work for unilateral U.S. disarmament and down played the threat of Soviet arms build-up. Close ties with the Women's International League for Peace and Freedom (pro-U.S. disarmament, anti-nuclear power) and the World Peace Council.

INNOCENTS—Several older organizations that formerly were truly liberal and had considerable prestige have come increasingly under the influence of the far left. These include *The American Civil Liberties Union, The American Friends Service Committee,* and the *Carnegie Endowment for International Peace.*

TRUE LIBERALS—Liberalism and the far left are anything but identical, but much of the far left's efforts are aimed at fostering the false impression that liberals support most of their goals. They do not.

*Social Democrats, U.S.A.,* noted for its anti-Communist stands, advocates the democratic road to Socialism. The *AFL/CIO,* the foremost bastion of political liberalism at home, is perhaps the strongest bulwark against Communism in the world.

40

The actions and stands of these organizations show that truly humanitarian liberals can be anti-Communist, making the groups of the Far Left Lobby even more conspicuous in their unwillingness to ever criticize Communist crimes.

# III. Proven Communist Agents in the Media—Singapore, Malaysia and France

Of all the countries in the free world, Singapore and Malaysia in recent years have uncovered the largest number of Communist agents in the media. These two governments have been especially vigilant against such subversion because their recent history has been marked by a bloody struggle against Communist insurgency. The Communist networks they have exposed during the last decade provide several valuable analogies to similar activities that may be going on in the United States.

In June, 1976, Singapore took into custody two leading journalists—the editor of the largest Malay-language newspaper, *Berita Harian Singapore,* and his assistant—accusing them of being Communist agents and using their paper to promote Communist propaganda. A few days later, the top journalist in the country, Abdul Samad Ismail (editor of Malaysia's prestigious *New Strait Times*) and his "accomplice," Samai Mohamad Amin, news editor of *Berita Harian* (Malaysia) were arrested and accused by the government of leading Malays into accepting Communism.

On September 1, Samad confessed on television that he had been a Communist for "three quarters of his life" and had been using his position to further the cause of Communism. Singapore announced that the two journalists they arrested, working in league with Samad, had been using their newspapers and influence among political leaders to soften the Malay environment for Communism.

Two weeks later, the Malaysian Security Service arrested two Deputy Ministers, who confessed on television to Communist activities and Soviet connections.

In February 1977, the Malaysian government arrested Chan Kien Sin, ex-editor-in-chief of a leading Chinese daily and Chief Executive Secretary of the Malaysian Chinese Association, a crucial group in the ruling National Front government. Chan confessed on TV, saying he had been a Communist for 30 years and had used his position on the paper to promote Communist propaganda. Later that month, Singapore announced the arrest of a group of pro-Communists, headed by lawyer Gopalkrishnan Raman. The public confessions of these people and correspondence found in their possession revealed the existence of a wide network of influence in the media at home and abroad, in universities, labor unions and religious bodies. Their methods for infiltrating opinion groups and influence on the media bear many resemblences to the work of the American Far Left organizations.

After his arrest in February 1977, Arun Senkuttuvan, correspondent for the *Far Western Economic Review,* the *Economist,* and the *Financial Times,* confessed that although not a Communist himself, he had been spreading anti-government, pro-Communist propaganda in cooperation with Raman's group.

Why did these Communists and their sympathizers make such complete confessions of their activities? One ominous explanation is that many of them simply feel that Communism is the wave of the future in Southeast Asia. They have often enunciated their version of the Domino Theory—that after the fall of Viet Nam, Laos, and Cambodia to the Communists, Thailand, Malaysia and Singapore would soon follow. They may have felt that after a few years in jail, under the relatively benign Singapore and Malaysian governments, they would be released (the Communists having taken over) and emerge as heroes of the revolution, with the prospect of prominent positions in the new regime.

These revelations of widespread Communist subversion in Singapore and Malaysia have been virtually ignored by the American media or simply treated as evidence of a repressive government, following the line that Raman and the others were attempting to promote. For example, the *NY Times* ran two long articles by a Singapore correspondent, David A. Andelman. The first, on June, 23, 1976, patronizingly treated the arrests of Samad and Amin as the result of the "frenzy" of anti-Communist fear in the Malaysian government and the fact that Prime Minister Lee of Singapore was "known to fear Mr. Samad as an extraordinarily able and *honest* journalist." (Emphasis added.) The second, a front page piece on April 4, 1977 reported on the arrests of Raman and his network as a "new campaign to repress dissent that has crippled the political opposition and a fledgling human rights movement" and a further effort to prop up

Lee's "dictatorship with a democratic facade."

The cases of Singapore and Malaysia indicate that the Communists will go to great lengths to successfully infiltrate and manipulate the media, even in relatively small countries like these. But in contrast to these countries, Western countries have paid little attention to subversion of the media. Our FBI is not even empowered to investigate such activities, and only one Western journalist, Pierre Charles Pathé, has ever been arrested (and sentenced to five years in prison) as an agent of influence for the Soviets in France. Arrested in 1979, while meeting with his KGB control, Pathé was accused of planting stories in the French press or in his own newsletter, *Synthesis* (financed by the Soviets), designed to sow discord among the NATO allies and discredit the Western secret services, especially the CIA. Over the 20 year period, he or his KGB ghostwriters wrote more than 100 such articles. Because of his many connections, he was also in a position to give the Soviets gossip about prominent journalists or officials for use in recruitment or blackmail.

Robert Moss, in the *London Daily Telegraph,* commented that "by putting Pathé behind bars, the French Court of State Security publicly recognized that this form of Soviet Covert action...may represent a danger equal to traditional espionage." *Paris Match* said, "In sending Pathé to jail for five years without considering his age or state of health, the judges firmly condemned him as a spy without him actually being one For them, Pathé is tangible proof that in France there are innumerable 'ants' of the KGB, 'ants' that are both insignificant and dangerous. These ants tirelessly and in little doses are the vehicles of false ideas.''

This case has been ignored by American media, but provides an ominous lesson for the U.S. as do the events in Singapore and Malaysia. If the Communists have spent enough time and effort over the past 20 years to subvert prominent journalists and government officials in France and these two small Southeast Asian countries, what efforts have they been making to influence the people controlling the media in a much more important target, the United States, their principle enemy? Have they been as successful as they were in France, Singapore and Malaysia? How many ''ants'' exist in the United States?

# IV. The Selling of Sihanouk and the Cambodian Communists

Among all the propaganda campaigns to be described in this book, the efforts on behalf of the Cambodian Communists and Prince Sihanouk had some of the most direct and disastrous effects on U.S. policy. And none of these campaigns had been so clearly revealed by later events to have been based on falsehoods. For five years (1970-75) American media were influenced by this propaganda to build up Prince Sihanouk in his Peking exile as an important factor in Cambodian politics, with whom the U.S. should negotiate to end the bloodshed. At the same time, many American commentators and media were portraying the Cambodian Communists as honest idealists, "gentle people," whose country was being ravaged by American bombs, and who, but for our violent opposition, would be willing to form a coalition government with other parties in their country.

What in fact was the true history?

During the 1960s, Sihanouk had attempted to steer a neutral course between the Communist subversion in his own country (the Khmer Rouge, headed by

Noun Chea and the notorious Pol Pot), backed by Viet Nam Communists and less directly by Soviets and Chinese, and the anti-Communist forces, the South Vietnamese, the U.S. and anti-Communists in his own government. This struggle was complicated by the fact that Cambodians of all beliefs feared and disliked the Vietnamese, who have been their enemies for centuries. In 1963, Sihanouk broke off diplomatic relations with the U.S. and South Vietnam and refused further U.S. aid. Under increasing pressure from the Communists, Sihanouk extended them great concessions in the way of transit rights and permission to use Cambodian territory against the Saigon government and the U.S. In the late '60's, the border areas of Cambodia became a de facto staging area for the North Vietnamese army, and by 1969, there were an estimated 40,000 North Vietnamese and Viet Cong along the borders. The whole border area became a rest and reassembly sanctuary for Communist troops. Though the presence of the hated Vietnamese was causing growing bitterness among the Cambodian people and many government officials in Phnom Penh, Sihanouk was unable to extricate himself from his agreements.

*The Bombing Campaign.* In 1968, Sihanouk proposed to Chester Bowles, visiting Phnom Penh, that the U.S. bomb the sanctuaries along the border, saying that he would not object as long as his acquiescence was kept secret. Early in 1969, President Nixon gave his approval. A major bombing campaign of the 10 mile border region followed, with elaborate precautions set up to prevent publicity and avoid embarrassing Sihanouk. He was still engaged in his manueverings with the North Vietnamese, China and the Soviets and it would have put him in an impossible position to admit he approved the raids. While the Communists did not complain publicly about the raids (they didn't want to admit that they had 40,000 North Vietnamese troups and Viet Cong inside Cambodia), they incorporated them into their propaganda in Cambodia, claiming U.S. air strikes were bringing death and destruction to the Cambodians. Although most Cambodians had been expelled from the sanctuary areas by the Communists and virtually none were killed by the bombings, the American media later bought this Communist propaganda completely in criticizing the bombing. They also misinterpreted the reasons all parties involved were reluctant to talk about the bombings publicly. In July 1973, the *NY Times* ran a front page story by Seymour Hersh critical of the bombing. The *Times* had sent a cable to Sihanouk asking whether he had been aware of the bombing. Sihanouk, deposed in 1970, had taken refuge in Peking, and in July, 1973, was visiting the ruler of North Korea. Sihanouk cabled the *Times* from the North Korean capital that he had not been aware of the bombing and that the raids "simply proved that the U.S. was preparing for the overthrow of his government." Seymour Hersh quoted the cable in his *Times* story, without questioning whether Sihanouk could have sent any other reply from a Communist capital.

The allegation that the U.S. had bombed a neutral country without its government's knowledge or consent grew to be one of the favorite examples of the American government's villainy among the anti-anti-Communists during the succeeding weeks and until the present. As late as 1977, no less an expert on U.S. foreign policy than Ben Bradlee, executive editor of the *Washington Post,* was quoted as saying that the news suppression that angered him the most during his career in Washington was the bombing of Cambodia. It is difficult to believe that sophisticated journalists like Bradlee and Hersh wouldn't know that the reason for secrecy was not to fool the American people, but to protect Sihanouk, and that they'd be taken in by such an obvious propaganda line.

After Sihanouk was deposed in 1970 and settled down in exile under the protection of the Chinese Communists, anti-anti-Communists in the U.S. blamed Nixon and Kissinger for not attempting to negotiate with Sihanouk to bring about his return to a "neutral" government. Facts now show that would have been impossible. Within two days of his arrival in Peking, without waiting for any U.S. approach, Sihanouk took sides with the North Vietnamese and turned violently against the U.S. and the new Lon Nol government. He issued a statement blaming his overthrow on the CIA and defending the Vietnamese Communists in Cambodia as resisting "American imperialism."

Between April 3 and 24, 1970, the North Vietnamese launched attacks on the Cambodian Republic's forces all across southern and eastern Cambodia in co-operation with the Viet Cong and Khmer Rouge. The U.S. saw the possibility of a Communist take-over of the entire country. Nixon decided on April 28 to order the "incursion" into the Cambodian border areas by South Vietnamese and American forces.

The later propaganda line was that our actions had somehow "driven the North Vietnamese deeper into

Cambodia," but the incursion was ordered *three weeks* after the North Vietnamese had themselves burst out of the border areas and started major operations further into Cambodia. The incursion led to the largest storm of protest of the entire Indo-China war, with accusations that we were invading a "neutral country" and expanding the war to include this small "gentle" people. The hysteria culminated in the Kent State riots and death of four students.

Kissinger's diplomacy in 1972 resulted in the Paris Peace Treaty of 1973 which called for a "cease fire" in South Vietnam, Laos and Cambodia. Lon Nol called for an immediate cease fire by his army, offering to negotiate a settlement, but the Communists refused and continued the fighting. Lon Nol was obliged to continue the war and asked for further U.S. aid, but the anti-war movement had become so powerful that the Congress forced Nixon to agree to a bill that would cut off all military operations by August 15. So the Cambodian Communists had to only hold out until that date. With this final cut-off of U.S. military support and reduced financial backing by Congress, the Cambodian government's ability to fight the Communists, with their backing from Hanoi, China and Russia, declined steadily. The Republic fell in April, 1975, shortly after the fall of Saigon.

The victorious Communists began to drive the population of Phnom Penh and other Cambodian cities and villages out at gun point—the sick, wounded, young, old—in an exodus that some commentators said was the most brutal since Ghengis Khan.

How was this tragic history reported by the media? Going back to 1970, a few months in that year, after Sihanouk was ousted, the *NY Times* took a neutral position. But on April 30, the *Times* wrote an editorial against any form of U.S. intervention, then joined in the general hysteria in the country when the incursion came. From then on, even after all the U.S. troops had been withdrawn on schedule, the *Times* reflected a growing negative attitude towards the Republican government and a tolerant attitude towards the Communists. The original incursion and our bombing, the only means the U.S. had after 1970 of supporting the small Cambodian army against the combined force of the Khmer Rouge and the North Vietnamese, were continually cited as the only reasons Cambodia was then at war. Commentators generally ignored the fact that the Cambodians themselves had overthrown Sihanouk and the North Vietnamese had attacked three weeks *before* the U.S. incursion.

Most of the "northeastern liberal press," which depends so much on the *Times* as a source, and the major broadcasting networks, echoed replays of the main Communist propaganda line. On May 6, a CBS correspondent in South Vietnam, interviewed Alpha Company, about to embark on fighting, asking: "Do you realize what can happen to you? Are you scared? Do you say the morale is pretty low in Alpha Company? What are you going to do?"

These questions prompted Senator Robert Dole to ask. "Does Freedom of the Press include the right to incite to mutiny? . . . . I believe a CBS reporter has come periously close to attempting to incite mutiny by playing on the emotions of soldiers just before they were to go into battle . . . . I can think of no other war in our history where this sort of thing would have been permitted."

By the beginning of 1975, with the fortunes of the Republican government declining, the clamor in the media increased, echoing the main Communist lines. On February 11, the *Times* ran an article by O. Edward Clubb, a former U.S. Foreign Services officer who has usually taken positions somewhat sympathetic to Communist regimes in Asia, which said that the "U.S. has always displayed an irrational opposition to revolutionary regimes" (like the Khmer Rouge). On February 13, there was a column by Anthony Lewis urging a coalition government with the Communists. Lon Nol offered to step aside on March 1 if that would bring peace, and on March 3, the *Times* ran an interview with Senator Mike Mansfield recommending a coalition government following Lon Nol's offer. In the same issue was a signed article by Prince Sihanouk, written at the *Times'* request. On February 25, Tom Wicker's column echoed the position that the war was all the fault of U.S. intervention. "It was the U.S. invasion of 1970 that brought full-scale war to a country that had been at peace, however uneasy. The real disaster is that of the gentle and unwarlike Cambodian people." On February 27, the *Times* ran an interview with Senator Mansfield in which he said letting Cambodia fall would "force the Cambodians to face up to their own future with no help or hindrance from the U.S., and that's the way it should be, and that's the way it's going to be!" On March 13, the *Times* published an article reporting a proposal of Senators Jackson and Mansfield to send Mansfield to Peking to negotiate a peace with Sihanouk. In the same issue was a long report from Phnom Penh by Sidney Schanberg examining the possibilities of a bloodbath if the Communists won and reporting that although there had been some stories of brutality from Communist occupied areas, these were probably exaggerated and that the bloodbath predicted by U.S. and Cambodian officials was unlikely.

A month later Phnom Penh had fallen and the massacre had started. Saigon surrendered to the North Vietnamese in the same month. For months after Phnom Penh's surrender, Communist propaganda played the line that this Communist victory was the victory of the people against U.S. imperialism and its lackeys; a line echoed by American media.

But the horrendous bloodbath that began immediately after the fall of Phnom Penh presented a major embarrassment for Communist propagandists. They had several alternatives. One was to deny it, which they tried to do for several months. But when denials were overwhelmed by the facts, this became difficult. The next alternative was to disassociate themselves from it. This the North Vietnamese and Soviets eventually did. Chinese Communists and their sympathizers, however, were left in the unpleasant position of having to defend the Khmer Rouge because they turned out to be one of the few buffers against the aggressive Soviets and North Vietnamese. But all Communists could and did agree to try to blame the horrors in Cambodia on American policy.

There is no direct evidence that Peking stimulated this effort. But there are indications that the stimulus did come from media and research people in the U.S. with sympathies for the Chinese Communists. And there is also the fact that the effort fit in directly with the pro-Khmer Rouge and pro-Chinese party line.

A key figure in this campaign was William Shawcross, a British journalist who reported on the Indo-China war for several years from Washington. Many of Shawcross's articles for the *Far Eastern Economic Review* in 1976 and 1977, and his book *Sideshow,* published in 1979, expounded the thesis that Nixon and Kissinger were responsible for the horrors in Cambodia. They had authorized the bombing of a "neutral country," they had "refused to negotiate with Sihanouk in Peking to bring about a neutral coalition in Phnom Penh," and finally they had authorized the invasion of this "neutral country," which "forced the North Vietnamese deeper into Cambodia and expanded the war." Shawcross's conclusions do not fit the facts summarized briefly earlier in this chapter. His book was severely critized by the liberal British weekly, *The Economist,* which said "This is not history. . . . Mr. Shawcross's book is free of (the right) questions, and free of answers too. It is too busy doing something else to be considered even remotely fair."

Nevertheless, Shawcross's theories on Cambodia were taken up eagerly by many in the media, who were anxious to blunt the impact of the horrors. Tom Wicker and Anthony Lewis echoed his lines in their columns in the *N. Y. Times.* The Educational Broadcasting Corporation interviewed Shawcross for TV. His book was recommended by Peter Osnos, Foreign Editor of the *Washington Post,* Walter Berkov in the *Cleveland Plain Dealer,* and Harrison Salisbury in the *Chicago Tribune. The New Yorker's* "Talk of the Town" joined in.

Whether or not deliberately, Shawcross provided another salvo in the Communist propaganda offensive to convince the American public that we should not interfere in *any* attempts by Communists to take over other countries.

Of all the case histories to be described in this volume, none will so clearly show the effects of Communist propaganda in emasculating our foreign policy.

Communist propaganda affected our media. The media in turn had profound impact on the opinions of students, intellectuals, and groups of opinion leaders, who in turn influenced Congress. At the same time, the Far Left Lobby organizations probably exerted direct influence on Congress.

Communist propaganda, however apparently had greater effect on the media and on Congress than it did on the general public. At the height of the hysteria in the media, in Congress, and in student bodies over the Cambodian incursion in 1970, the Gallup Poll found that 50% of the people approved of the Government's policy in Cambodia, 35% disapproved, and 15% had no opinion.

In retrospect, our abandonment of Cambodia was a disgraceful retreat from American honor and commitments to defend the freedom of countries facing aggression. This small country was unified in its fear and dislike of the Vietnamese and abhorrence of Communism. The Cambodians appealed for aid and fought hard by themselves, tying down large Communist forces for five years. Yet we spurned them. The actions of Congress in cutting off our aid marked a tragic abandonment of the principles declared by President John F. Kennedy in his inaugural address in

1961: "We shall pay any price, bear any burden, meet any hardship" to defend freedom around the world.

## The Flip-Flop on Cambodia

After the Communist conquest of Cambodia, many American media exhibited some strange and significant behaviour.

One of the most convincing signs that an organizations is being influenced by foreign propaganda is when it displays a sudden shift in opinion coinciding exactly with a shift in policy of a foreign country. This type of switch in response to the Communist Party line is called "Zig-zag Parallelism." Communist propaganda and the reaction of American media to the Cambodian horrors went through two phases, providing striking examples of such parallelism. From 1975-1977, the reports were ignored or discounted by many in the media who had been sympathetic to the Khmer Rouge and opposed U.S. assistance to the Cambodian Republic government. In 1978, a shift took place. Indo-China became the scene of violent confrontation between countries which became Communist after 1975. The cooperation that existed among the Soviet, Vietnamese, Cambodian, and Chinese Communists until their victories in April 1975, had fallen apart by 1978. By mid-1978, there was an overt split between the Cambodians backed by the Chinese on one side and the Vietnamese backed by the Soviets in the other.

This was reflected abruptly in the propaganda. As late as January 3, 1978, Radio Moscow was still following a line friendly to the Khmer Rouge, broadcasting a New Year's messsage of support to the Cambodian people. Within two days, the tone began to change. Radio Moscow started to air stories of "border tensions" between Cambodia and Viet Nam. It quoted the Vietnamese ambassador as saying that Viet Nam was resisting Cambodian aggression. On January 12, the World Peace Council, always a barometer of Soviet foreign policy, declared that it "supports the Vietnamese position." On January 19, Radio Moscow said "the Vietnamese radio asks for peace. The Cambodian radio fans hysteria." On January 26, the Vietnamese radio declared that Viet Nam "refutes the Cambodian charge that Vietnam is attempting to carry out its Federation Plan." By March, Radio Moscow reported the "Cambodian failure to respond to Vietnamese proposals for negotiations," and March 3, 1978, Radio Moscow broadcast a long commentary from *Novoye Vremya* on the "Medieval Barbarities Characterizing Cambodian Actions." From then on all gloves were off and attacks from Radio Moscow and Hanoi on Cambodia became as fierce as they had even been against the American "imperialists" in Viet Nam.

This shift was reflected almost immediately in the American media. Although no direct evidence of cause and effect is available, the coincidence is remarkable. With the Cambodian holocaust ongoing for almost three years, there was no more reason for discovering it in 1978 than there had been a year before. After early 1977, additional evidence poured in, with one unimaginable horror piled on top of another, but the evidence differed only in degree rather than in kind from previous clear indications that horrors had taken place. Thus, the only new factor as of early 1978 was the Soviet Union's new attitude. When the pro-Soviet elements in the Far Left Lobby switched instantly, this somehow made it respectable for those who look to the far left for clues to join in.

Anthony Lewis's columns in the *Times* for the first time admitted the horrors, although one column quoted William Shawcross in attempting to place much of the blame on American policy. Coverage of human rights violations in Cambodia increased considerably in the *Times,* with 48 mentions in 1978 compared to 34 in 1977. In the *Washington Post,* such mentions increased from 10 in 1977 to 29 in 1978. In July 1978, more than a year after they had been published and become best-sellers, the *Post* finally reviewed two major books on the Cambodian holocaust, Barron and Paul's *Murder of a Gentle Land* and Father Francois Ponchard's *Cambodia—Year Zero.*

TV mentions of the massacres also increased considerably, reaching a climax of sorts on June 8 when CBS broadcast a program anchored by Ed Bradley featuring an all-star cast of "experts" on Cambodia, including Gareth Porter, William Shawcross, and Tiziano Terzani. All of these now confirmed that horrendous massacres had in fact occurred, with Porter completely reversing the position he had taken before the House Subcommittee.

The only exception on the program was Daniel Burstein of the Communist Party (Marxist-Leninist), the Chicago-based party that supports China and opposes the Soviet Union. Burstein is editor of the party's weekly newspaper, *The Call,* and had recently returned from a visit to China and Cambodia, where he and two associates were the first Americans admitted since the Khmer Rouge victory. He testified rather lamely under sharp questioning by Ed Bradley that all reports of brutality in Cambodia were exaggerated.

The climactic and most dramatic shift in viewpoint came in August 1978 from Senator George McGovern. At a Senate Foreign Relations Committee hearing, McGovern called on the State Department to recommend an international military force to "knock the Cambodian regime out of power." McGovern had run for president in 1972 on a platform of American withdrawal from Indo-China and cessation of support for the anti-Communist governments there. In 1974, with the Communists winning in Cambodia, he declared that the Cambodians "should be left to settle their own affairs." Now he said military intervention was justified because of evidence that more than 2.5 million out of Cambodia's population of more than 6 million had died from starvation, disease, or execution since the Communist victory. His statement evoked bitter comments from the *Wall Street Journal* and others who had supported American resistance to the Communists in Indo-China. Why, they asked, had McGovern not foreseen the dangers of a Communist victory before it was too late?

Thus, from mid-1978 onwards, almost immediately after the USSR began opposing the Khmer Rouge, the only people defending the Cambodian regime were those with obvious ties to Peking. Burstein and the CP (ML) were the most extreme examples. Then in

December 1978 occurred the strange visit of three Western journalists to Cambodia, the first and only reporters to be admitted by the Pol Pot regime after Burstein's group.

These included Elizabeth Becker of the *Washington Post,* Richard Dudman of the *St. Louis Post Dispatch,* and Malcolm Caldwell, a British instructor from London University. All had shown earlier evidence of partiality towards the Chinese and Cambodian Communists. Elizabeth Becker had been a *Post* correspondent in Phnom Penh in 1973 and 1974, when she wrote articles generally critical of the Cambodian Republic's government and sympathetic to the Khmer Rouge. Back in Washington as a *Post* writer, she showed the same sympathy for the Khmer Rouge even after the evidence of their brutality became overwhelming during 1977. In January of 1978, Miss Becker attended an American Security Council press conference at which a Cambodian refugee, Pin Yathay, presented one of the most authenticated eye-witness accounts of the massacres. Pin, a civil engineer, escaped after surviving 26 months in Cambodia and witnessing the death of all of his family. He told "many macabre incidents. . . . The starving people ate the flesh of dead bodies during this acute famine. Now I will tell you a story that I lived myself. . . a teacher who ate the flesh of her own dead sister. She was later caught and beaten to death, in front of the whole village, as an example, with her child crying beside her." Halfway through this press conference, Elizabeth Becker walked out. She was helped into her coat by an employee of the American Security Council, who heard her exclaim, "I have heard enough of this junk." The *Post* failed to carry a story of this press conference.

Richard Dudman had also shown a strong partiality for the Cambodian and Chinese Communists. In 1970, while covering the war in Cambodia, he and some other correspondents were captured by the Khmer Rouge. Dudman was released after six weeks, and there is evidence that he was freed because of the intervention of anti-war activists in the U.S., who considered him an ally. He later wrote a book about his experience in captivity, tending to favor the Khmer Rouge and saying nothing about their brutality, which was becoming evident even after 1974.

Malcolm Caldwell of London University was a member of the British Labor Party, but known to be active in London's Maoist Communist circles. In 1977, he was implicated in the public TV confessions of a Communist-agent-of-influence in Singapore, G. Raman. (See Chapter III.) Raman had met Caldwell while studying in London in the 1960s. Caldwell persuaded him to recruit agents in Singapore to spread propaganda and to gather information unfavorable to the Singapore government, information Caldwell used to try to discredit Singapore in European media and the Socialist International. Caldwell had also lectured and written articles defending the Pol Pot regime.

These three arrived at Phnom Penh by way of Peking in December, 1978. A Cambodian radio broadcast quoted Caldwell as saying, "I have been trying for years to create more sympathy for your country in Britain. And I know that I shall be able to carry on this work much more successfully as the result of having the opportunity to visit your country." They stayed for two weeks and were given guided tours around the country, finishing with an interview with Pol Pot himself. On the early morning before they were to leave, three gunmen broke into their house. Caldwell was killed. Dudman narrowly escaped when a gunman missed him from only 20 feet. Elizabeth Becker escaped by hiding in her bath tub. The assassins were believed to be members of the pro-Vietnamese underground in Cambodia. Their motives were either to discredit the Pol Pot government by showing that they could not protect their own guests, or to take revenge on pro-Pol Pot journalists.

Becker and Dudman returned to the U.S. via Peking and wrote a series of articles frankly describing Cambodia's desolation: Phnom Penh was like ''Pompeii without the ashes,'' said Dudman and there were signs of hunger, and a cowed and dispirited population. They also admitted that they had been given a Potemkin tour and were not free to interview whom they pleased. Yet they somehow managed to conclude with favorable impressions. Dudman argued that ''The physical conditions may well have improved for many peasants and former urban workers, . . . the new leader are not fanatical madmen . . . the crash evacuation of Phnom Penh may well have been essential to resume food production. Cambodia is in the midst of one of the world's great housing programs.'' Becker concluded that the production figures given them could not be too misleading and that ''the system was working.'' The system was working indeed, if its purpose was to destroy a people and a culture.

Both these journalists reported that the Vietnamese forces in the area had been repulsed the year before and were now weaker than before. But within a week, they were proved wrong. The Vietnamese launched their long-planned final invasion and drove through to Phnom Penh by January 7. The Pol Pot government was forced to flee to the jungles.

The Vietnamese set up their puppet regime under Heng Samrin. In the first weeks it appeared that any government, even one sponsored by the hated Vietnamese, would be preferable to the murderous Pol Pot regime. But as the months wore on and the guerilla fighting with the Pol Pot remnants continued, the Vietnamese and their puppets refused to allow imports of foods to the contested areas. So another cycle of starvation and bloodshed started for the unfortunate gentle people of Cambodia.

The reactions of American media and opinion leaders since the fall of Cambodia to the Khmer Rouge in April 1975 provided several clear cases of Zig-zag Parallelism." Columnist Anthony Lewis, research analysts William Goodfellow and Gareth Porter, and Senator George McGovern defended the Pol Pot regime long after the time when the evidence of their brutality was overwhelming. Then when the Soviets and Vietnamese switched from support of to opposition to Pol Pot, most such people also made the same abrupt change. A similar change took place in the coverage of most of the major media.

*The New York Times* editorial page denounced the horrors soon after they became evident, and Henry Kamm reported them in detail from Southeast Asia, but the rest of the *Times* news columns and Op Ed page showed the same swing from indifference or disbelief to strong denunciation. The *Washington Post* and the major TV networks also made a similar abrupt shift in early 1978.

Why was it only after the Soviet propaganda machine suddenly "discovered" Khmer Route brutality in 1978 that many U.S. media and opinion leaders allowed themselves to do the same? And why was it that only the pro-Peking members of the Far Left Lobby desperately clung to their defenses of Pol Pot and his cohorts? The zigs and zags of U.S. media and "intellectuals" and their correspondence with the twists and turns of Soviet and Chinese propaganda are indeed enlightening. We like to boast of our freedom of the press, but our press may be far less free than we think.

# V. Whitewashing the North Vietnamese

The worldwide propaganda in support of the struggle by the North Vietnamese against the United States was one of the largest campaigns in history. Once the U.S. had withdrawn from Indochina, the propaganda had two new objectives: 1) to persuade the U.S. and other democracies to grant political recognition and economic aid, and 2) to convince the American public that our involvement in Viet Nam had been a gigantic mistake, that we had been opposing a sincere movement for national liberation, and therefore that, in the future, we should not "interfere in other countries' internal affairs." Or to use a popular media phrase, we should not try to be "the policeman for the world." The first objective was of primary interest to the Vietnamese who were facing tremendous economic problems. The second was a particular aim of the Soviets. By taking advantage of this "first defeat ever suffered by the U.S.," the Soviet propaganda could do much to convince the American public that we should never again become involved in such foreign adventures.

This scenario of the non-interventionist propaganda

line had been promoted in the U.S. for many years before 1975 by those who wanted the U.S. to quit the war. In 1972, Senator Ted Kennedy said the U.S. should get out of Viet Nam and "let the Vietnamese settle their own problems," causing Singapore's brilliant, sharp-tongued prime minister, Lee Kwan Yew, to say that in view of the massive Communist interference in Viet Nam on the other side, Kennedy must be "out of his mind." Statements such as Kennedy's began to prove false almost immediately after the Communist take-over. The North Vietnamese set up a typically authoritarian Communist regime in Saigon. Though given token titles, southern leaders of the Viet Cong gradually dropped out of sight. All former members of the South Vietnamese Army, government officials and those who had done any business with the government or the Americans were required to report for "re-education." Persecution of religious groups began. In November 1975, 12 Buddhist monks burned themselves to death in protest against government repression, an event virtually ignored by the media. The Catholic Church also came under severe pressure, and by summer of 1977, there were 300 priests and 6 bishops in prison.

A massive system of prisons and "re-education" camps was set up all over South Viet Nam and extended into the North, like the Soviet Gulag Archipelago on a smaller scale. Father Gelinas, a Jesuit priest who lived in Viet Nam for 20 years and remained in Saigon for 15 months after the Communist conquest, estimated a minimum of 300,000 prisoners in 1977. Other estimates ranged as high as 800,000, and refugees reported that large numbers of "re-education center" prisoners were slowly being starved to death.

The Soviet and Vietnamese propaganda machine, of course, presented a much more attractive picture of Viet Nam after the fall of Saigon in 1975. But in order for the propagandists to argue convincingly that it had massive support when such large numbers of people were fleeing desperately, in 1975-76, they waged a campaign against the refugees, following two somewhat contradictory lines: most of the refugees were misguided and would want to return; most of them were the scum of Vietnamese society and lackeys of the Americans. These lines appeared first in publications of the Far Left Lobby and its sympathetic allies. For example, in April 1975, the American Friends Service Committee distributed a flyer, "Vietnam: Why the Refugees?" by Edward Block, who was affiliated with a number of Far Left organizations in attacking the U.S. effort in Viet Nam. The flyer's point is that the refugees were not fleeing from Communism but from fear of additional American bombing. But this assertion did not explain why the refugees were leaving the "safe" Communist areas for the dangerous areas held by a crumbling government! Communist propaganda, and its American echoes, could only portray the refugees as irrational, panic-striken people. But after the fall of Saigon and the complete cessation of fighting, it was unmistakable that the refugees actually preferred the risk of death at sea to life in the new socialist paradise. The depth of the campaign in 1975 was reached with Herblock's cartoon in the *Washington Post,* showing the Statue of Liberty with a worried expression on her face, looking at a procession of seedy Vietnamese entering the country, and captioned, "Give

me your drug pushers, pimps, prostitutes, your torturers and embezzlers.''

Direct Communist propaganda (printed materials
and broadcasts from Moscow, Hanoi and Peking)
sought to depict Vietnam as a place full of brave efforts to restore a war-damaged country and bring
about national reconciliation. In the U.S., the Far Left
Lobby echoed this line. A typical example was Don
Luce of Clergy and Laity Concerned, who testified before the House Subcommittee on International Organizations in June 1977, that he had visited Viet Nam in
April and came back "with a very optimistic feeling
about a society that is working very hard to rebuild.''
This line was reflected in the American TV networks
and liberal northeastern media, from the time of the
Communist victory through 1977, ignoring the testi-
monies of the many refugees coming out of Viet Nam
who could give authoritative evidence of the horrors.
By late 1976, when evidence of brutal oppression in
Viet Nam was becoming overwhelming, it began to
have some influence on humanitarians in the U.S., including many who had been anti-war agitators. The
Fellowship of Reconciliation, a pacifist organization in
New York and Amsterdam, which had been active in
opposing the war, began circulating a letter within the
peace movement, expressing concern over reports of
large numbers of prisoners, maltreatment and a violation of human rights. It asked for permission for neutral organizations like Amnesty International or the
U.N. to make on-site inspections. The 112 signers included many former anti-war activists such as Joan
Baez and Daniel Ellsberg, and liberals, including Kay
Boyle and ACLU founder, Roger Baldwin. Attempts

were made to present the letter privately and without publicity to the Vietnamese U.N. observer, but Mr. Thi ignored all letters and phone calls. As a last resort, the group called a press conference for December 29, 1976, and released the letter publicly. Between the first discussion of the letter and the public announcement, there was tremendous pressure on the signers to withdraw their names. Here the separations between true humanitarians and dedicated pro-Communists was most evident. Anti-war activists most closely connected with the Far Left Lobby, led by Gareth Porter of the Indo-China Resource Center, not only refused to sign but vigorously attempted to prevent publication of the letter.

In 1977 and '78, conditions in Viet Nam worsened—two poor harvests (blamed on the after-effects of U.S. defoliation, "flooding," "drought"), low rice rations, hunger and even starvation—causing an increase in the flood of refugees.

In the 1975-76 period, the evidence of tyranny in Viet Nam had drawn little mention in the print media and was almost ignored by TV. In 1978, there was some pickup in the media but most mentioned referred to the ethnic Chinese refugees from Viet Nam. This raises the question as to whether some of this attention was stimulated by persons having sympathy for the Chinese Communists, who were engaged in a major confrontation with Viet Nam. It was at this time that Hoang Van Hoan, Vietnamese politboro member and a close friend of Ho Chi Minh, defected to Peking in a disagreement over Vietnamese policy towards China, issuing statements critical of the Vietnamese tilt towards the Soviets and persecutions of their Chinese minority. Still hard core ultra-liberals and the Far Left Lobbyists continued to paint a favorable picture of Viet Nam. In the August 3, 1979 *NY Times,* the first of six articles on Viet Nam by Seymour Hersh appeared. Hersh had spent 10 days in Viet Nam, one of the few American correspondents to be admitted since the early months of Communist rule. His articles seemed to reflect his gratitude for this favor, painting a universally rosy picture of conditions there.

True liberals, however, were becoming increasingly disillusioned. In May, 1979, a number of those who had signed the 1977 appeal to the Vietnamese composed another letter. The leading spirit was Joan Baez and the letter more outspoken. Again, the hard-core members of the Far Left refused to be associated. Attacks on Joan Baez and the other signers appeared, including an ad in the *NY Times* (June 24, 1979) headlined "The Truth About Viet Nam." In comparison to similar pro-Vietnamese appeals of earlier years there is a complete absence of any of the well-known idealists and a large number of the signers are known Communists. It appears that backers of Viet Nam have finally exhausted the support of the large number of humanitarian liberals who were seduced for years into backing the policies of this tyrannical regime, undermining U.S. policy and encouraging the final collapse of the South Vietnamese government. Jean Lacouture, a French liberal journalist who reported on the Viet Nam war for *La Monde,* publicly confessed his "shame for having contributed to the installation of one of the most repressive regimes history has ever known," adding that he and other journalists were "intermediaries for a lying and criminal propaganda—

ingenuous spokesmen for a tyranny in the name of liberty." How many Lacoutures still exist in U.S. media today? How many American reporters or TV commentators don't realize they are being used as "intermediaries for a lying and criminal propaganda?" What is the next target for Communist conquest, or the next campaign to undermine American security or economic progress at home that they are being manipulated into helping? Though the veil of illusion on the nature of the Vietnamese Communists was being swept away, the second objective of the propaganda campaign, to convince us that the U.S. made a great mistake in interfering in another country's internal affairs, was still having disastrous influence. When anti-Communist factions in Angola and Ethiopia appealed to the U.S. for help against the Communists, Congress refused. In Angola, the Communists, with massive Cuban and Russian support, won. Ethiopia fell to the Communists after extremely bloody fighting that went almost unnoticed in the U.S. and the entire Horn of Africa was dominated by the Communists.

American isolationism was succinctly expressed by a scholar who should have known better, Arthur Schlesinger, Jr.: "Six months ago, most Americans had never heard of the Horn of Africa, and now the government is creating panic that this might affect our interests." (Shades of 1938 in England when Chamberlain's followers asked who had ever heard of the Sudentenland.)

# VI. The Campaign Against the Agency for International Development

The Agency for International Development (AID) grew out of President Truman's 1949 Point Four Program, which called for a "bold new program for making the benefits of our scientific advance and industrial progress available for the improvement and growth of underdeveloped areas." AID was set up in 1961 to take over this and all other foreign assistance programs, administering a large number of projects in medicine, education, land reform, agriculture and labor relations in underdeveloped countries.

The Communists began sniping at these activities almost immediately. Soviet publications and Radio Moscow broadcasts to underdeveloped countries attacked the program as an American device for penetrating "colonial" countries and seizing control of them after the other "imperialist" powers had pulled out. The campaign became more ferocious after 1966 as the Viet Nam War heated up and AID became more active in Indochina in humanitarian fields. American media attacked AID's program to advise the underdeveloped countries in Public Safety methods. In 1962, President

Kennedy founded the International Police Academy in Washington, saying the police constitute "the first line of defense against subversion in troubled Third World countries." The police training program was an attractive target for Communist propaganda, which accused AID of training people in how to make deadly booby traps and torture civilians. Characteristic of modern Communist propaganda campaigns, the propaganda began to originate in U.S. media as well as in the Soviet organs themselves. On October 8, 1973, Jack Anderson's column alleged that "Bomb and booby trap experts from the CIA have been quietly training foreign police to make explosives devices. . . . The cloak and dagger professors are on loan from the CIA to the AID." Anderson fails to make clear that the course was designed to teach the police how to combat bombings and booby traps, not create them. On August 3, 1974, Anderson reported that "students at the International Police Academy. . .have developed some chilling views about torture tactics." Accuracy in Media's investigation found that Anderson's researcher had taken quotes completely out of context from the essays of six students, who in fact, opposed the use of torture. AIM complained to the National News Council, an organization founded to monitor the media, and the Council upheld AIM's complaint, stating the Anderson's column was "biased and inaccurate." However, the charges that AID was training foreign torturers had direct repercussions.

On August 10, 1970, the body of an American was found in the back seat of a stolen car on a street in Montevideo, Uruguay. Blood was dripping through the floor boards. The man had been shot twice in the head and twice in the body. His eyes were bandaged, and his arms were pitted by 16 needle punctures. His left arm-pit had deep bruises, close to a gun-shot wound. This was the body of Dan A. Mitrione, employed by AID to teach police techniques to the Uruguayan government and kidnapped eleven days earlier by the Tupamaros, a large terrorist organization in Uruguay. Mitrione had been tortured and then tried by a Tupamaros "People's Court," accused of being a CIA or FBI agent teaching the Uruguayan police methods of torture and repression, and then executed.

Three years later, his story became the theme of an even more sophisticated Communist propaganda effort, the movie, *State of Siege,* co-authored by the noted director, Constantin Gavras (Costa-Gavras, the "Alfred Hitchock of the Left"), and an Italian Communist, Franco Solinas. *State of Siege* portrays the Uruguayan government as tyrannical and the Tupamaros as clean-cut humanitarian idealists. Both are gross distortions. Uruguay in 1970 was one of the most liberal democracies in the world, and the Tupamaros, a mixture of idealists, hard-nosed terrorists, and common criminals. Founded in the early 1960s, the Tupamaros (an organization of more than 1,000 members) committed its first murder by 1966 and by 1970 had already killed nine people. Mitrione was their tenth victim. By the time they were crushed, the Tupamaros had caused thousands of deaths.

The movie implies that Uruguay was already under martial law and in a "state of siege" in 1970, but this was not the case. Not until three years later, one day after the Tupamaros had murdered five government officials, did the Parliament declare martial law. By that time, the Tupamaros had killed 45 people.

The principal message of *State of Siege* was that the United States had cooperated with the Uruguayan authorities in this tyrannical regime, with Mitrione assisting them as a CIA agent under AID cover, teaching the police refined methods of torture. This became a principal theme in the Communist propaganda campaign against AID; that it was training the police forces of repressive regimes in Third World countries in torture techniques.

This movie was filmed in Chile during the pro-Communist Allende regime. Offered to the Chilean government, it was turned down as being too obviously a Communist propaganda documentary. Nevertheless, it was shown in many art cinemas in the U.S. and got several favorable reviews, including one from Vincent Canby in the *N.Y. Times*.

Dr. Ernest W. Lefever, at the Brookings Institution in Washington in the 1960's, conducted a 15 country field trip survey of AID's Public Safety Program and found no evidence of the torture charge. Nevertheless, in 1974, both houses passed a bill to eliminate the entire program.

The Communist campaign's most telling effect on U.S. media was to influence them in later years to ignore the good works of AID. Although there was no mention in the *Times,* from 1968 on, of AID accomplishments in Viet Nam nor of the hundreds of AID advisors who had given years of sacrificial service in Viet Nam, there were bitter attacks and on January 15, 1978, the *Times* ran a story on a single AID official who had resigned and had something negative to say.

The result of the Communist propaganda campaign against AID, echoed by far leftists and re-echoed by American media was to reduce public support for such activities abroad, lead to further doubts in the minds of the American people about the aims and activities of our government and its leaders, and create an image of AID as an organization that encouraged torture, bombings and other nefarious activities. In fact, AID was devoted to the most humanitarian activities in medicine, education, labor relations and land reform, and reflected some of the highest ideals of the American people both in its policies and character and devotion of its employees.

# VII. The Campaign Against Vietnamese Labor Unions

The Communist campaign against Vietnamese labor unions provides one of the clearest case histories of the success of propaganda in causing bias in American media. It is also a good example in microcosm of the Communist's world-wide offensive against free unions, partly by promotion of dummy Communist unions, and partly by an all-encompassing propaganda effort.

Labor unions were active in Viet Nam for decades, well before U.S. involvement began. Under French rule from 1862 to 1941, the large class of laborers and tenant farmers rebelled against the French in 1940, with the slogan, "Land to the Tillers, Freedom for the Workers, Independence for Viet Nam." One of the leaders of this revolt was Tran Quoc Buu, a schoolteacher who later became the father of the labor union movement in Viet Nam.

Under French rule, union membership was forbidden for Vietnamese nationals although permitted for Frenchmen. Buu started a Vietnamese labor confederation in 1949, with the cooperation of French labor organizers. By 1954, the federation, the CVT (Confederation Vietnamienne de Travail), had joined the International Labor Organization and counted 100,000 members.

After division of the country in 1954, when the Ho Chi Minh Government took over the North, about half of the CVT members were in the North. The Communists persecuted labor leaders in the North, executing or jailing some, forcing others to flee. The free union movement was wiped out and only dummy Communist unions remain to this day.

In South Viet Nam, the Diem government was friendly to labor for a while and union membership grew to about 500,000. Diem began to repress the unions, but conditions improved under the Thieu administration. The Thieu government carried out a major land reform program in 1970, stimulated partly by the Tenant Farmers Federation (with 330,000 members) which practically wiped out the serious farm tenancy problem in South Viet Nam.

ILO data on work stoppage and man hours lost from 1967 to 1972 shows that Vietnamese unions were more active than any others in Asia, a clear indication that these were not dummy unions.

The Communists began waging a major propaganda campaign against the CVT after 1965, as the war heated up. By 1970, Buu was being attacked more by Radio Hanoi than any other individual in South Viet Nam, except Thieu. The Communists regarded free unions as a major threat to their attempts to undermine the society of the country by portraying the Thieu government as a tyranny and Buu as nothing but a CIA agent, plotting to impose restrictions on labor for the benefit of American imperialists and their lackeys.

The CVT was getting well publicized assistance from AID in training and techniques, and it would not be surprising if AID in turn fed information to the CIA, but it would be ludicrous to say that Buu was "nothing but" a CIA agent. No CIA or AID backing could produce a trade union confederation of 500,000 members, and the CVT had a membership of at least 100,000 in 1954, before the U.S. had much direct interest in South Viet Nam and certainly before the CIA or AID knew much about Vietnamese unions.

The Communists also carried out an assassination campaign against the CVT. More than 100 free union organizers were assassinated from 1960 to 1974, and three attempts were made on Buu's life. This was denied by the Communists before the fall of Saigon, but Tiziano Terzani, a pro-Communist correspondent of the German magazine, *Der Spiegel,* has now revealed, in his book on the subject, *Giai Phong (Liberation),* that the attempts on Buu's life were the work of a Viet Cong assassination team. The leader of the team told Terzani that the Viet Cong tried to make it appear that the attempts on Buu's life were the work of the South Vietnamese military, and one member of the team was thrown out of the Communist party for confessing publicly on TV that it was the work of the Communists. Terzani, whose book echoes all of the Communist propaganda lines (and received a favorable review in the *New York Times),* also calls Buu a "CIA agent" and says that the CVT was financed by "various organs of the 'International Right'." One wonders if Terzani really believes that the AFL-CIO is part of the

International Right.

Effects on the U.S. media: A few mentions of Buu and the CVT as CIA agents in the radical press, including the Hayden-Fonda *Focal Point* magazine and *Ramparts.* Richard Dudman of the *St. Louis Post Dispatch,* in a *New Republic* article, "AFL/CIO as Paid Propagandists," refers to "Agent Meany," and criticizes the activities of the CVT in Viet Nam. In the famous Marchetti-Marks book, *The CIA and the Cult of Intelligence,* several paragraphs were deleted at the insistence of the CIA. One deletion immediately follows Buu's name, and would seem to imply that Marchetti is claiming that Buu was an "agent." (Among other mistakes, Marchetti gives Buu the wrong middle name.) But the major effect on American media of the Communist campaign, as in the case of AID, was to cause errors of omission, resulting in the labor union movement in Viet Nam being virtually ignored.

A check of *The Reader's Guide to Periodical Literature* shows that the 124 publications indexed there contained not a single article on the CVT or Buu throughout the entire history of U.S. involvement in Viet Nam, from 1955 to 1975. Another check, through its index for this twenty year period, indicates the same is true of the *New York Times.* Two one-inch stories appeared during this period: one when Buu barely escaped assassination and the second when he attacked the U.S. mistakes in Viet Nam. Then in 1974, the *Times* finally devoted one full column to Buu when he openly denounced Thieu for the first time. The *Times* apparently only found Vietnamese labor unions newsworthy when they could be used for negative coverage of the South Viet Nam government.

There was good coverage in the labor press—AFL/CIO publications, *The Machinist,* etc. and Victor Riesel's columns—but nothing in the general media. Considerable treatment of Buu and the CVT does appear, however, in *The Politics of Massacre,* by Professor Charles A. Joiner of Temple University (Philadelphia, 1974), the most complete study of South Vietnamese politics.

The general media's neglect of labor unions in Viet Nam would be comparable to their covering American politics and business over the past 20 years, without mentioning the AFL/CIO or George Meany. In fact, they were missing a rather dramatic and moving story, of the struggles of Buu and his associates to build up a free labor union movement in spite of French Imperialism, Communist subversion, and a major war within their own country.

Finally in 1975 came the fall of Saigon. Three days later, the *Times* ran a front page story on a parade of "2,000 members" of the Communist labor union organization in Saigon. Of all the evidences of the effects of Communist propaganda on the *Times,* certainly this is one of the clearest. Any journalist with an elementary knowledge of world labor union affairs knows that unions in Communist countries are simply another instrument of Government control of the population. Any union which tries to assert its independence is quickly snuffed out or emasculated. Communism, which claims to be the voice of the workers, simply cannot afford to allow a real and independent workers' voice. For the *Times* editors to ignore free unions in Viet Nam for twenty years and then to front-page the first demonstration by a Communist "union" is a startling example of bias.

The campaign against Vietnamese labor unions and its success among American media, is a clear example of the continuing world-wide Communist effort to destroy free labor unions by propaganda, or by penetration, or physical force, and to substitute their own dummy unions. Poland is the most recent example, but this has been conscious Communist practice since the days of Lenin. When the Comintern was founded in 1921, the 21 conditions which Communist parties had to accept to join included not one word about improving the lot of the working class, but instructions to (1) infiltrate and attempt to capture existing trade unions, and (2) propagandize for a break of national trade unions from the existing International of Trade Unions in favor of a projected new International of Unions (an organization which would be Communist dominated).

After WW II, there was considerable hope in the West that the Soviets had given up ideas of world domination and stood for the rights of the workers. The World Federation of Trade Unions (WFTU) was founded in 1945. Disillusionment set in soon, and in 1949, non-Communist trade unions withdrew and founded the International Confederation of Free Trade Unions (ICFTU). The WFTU has since devoted a major effort to attacking the ICFTU. In the United States, the organization with the closest ties to the WFTU is Trade Unionists for Action and Democracy, which regularly hosts visits by "trade union" officials from the Soviet Union.

Soviet efforts to promote subversion through trade unions have grown greatly since WW II. There is a special department in the KGB on labor affairs, a counterpart in the Propaganda Ministry and KGB labor specialists in Soviet embassies in most major countries.

Red unions have been prominent in most Communist attempts to seize power, as in Chile under Allende, where the Communist unions were financed from Moscow much more liberally than the free trade unions were supported by the U.S. In the struggle for Portugal in 1975 and '76, the Communists almost succeeded in taking over the only large labor federation in the country, thanks to millions of dollars poured into the country by the KGB.

The Soviets made an energetic effort to restore the relations between the WFTU and labor unions in democratic countries by a vigorous propaganda campaign on the need for labor solidarity. The head of the Russian trade union organization spearheading this drive (the All Union Central Council of Trade Unions) was ex-KGB director, Alexander Shelepin, a man without previous labor union experience. He had some success in improving relations with Western union officials. But during a London visit in 1975, newspapers published the fact that his KGB duties had led to involvement in a murder in Germany. After hostile demonstrations by British anti-Communist unionists, he was forced to return to Moscow early and soon removed from his "trade union" post.

In the 1960's and '70s, AID, in cooperation with the AFL/CIO, carried out an education and assistance program for new or weak unions in other countries. Working through the African-American Labor Center, based in New York City, the Asian-American Free Labor Institute, and the American Institute for Free Labor Development, AID provided much valuable support to unions in Viet Nam, Indonesia, Thailand, the Philippines, Zaire and elsewhere in Africa, and Chile, Brazil, Mexico and Uruguay in Latin America.

These American efforts stimulated vigorous countermeasures by the Soviet propaganda apparatus. In the U.S. efforts began that were the first seeds of the later massive assault on the CIA. In 1966, Victor Reuther of the United Auto Workers, a bitter rival of George Meany and the AFL/CIO, charged that the CIA was operating through the AFL/CIO labor institutes. Senators Eugene McCarthy and J. William Fulbright picked up this charge and attempted to get a Senate committee to investigate the CIA. Though their attempt failed in 1966, some of the dirt stuck, and this became a favorite theme of Communist propaganda. Any anti-Communist union in another part of the world from then on could be accused of being a "CIA tool" and an "agent of the American monopolies and multi-nationals."

The massive Communist campaign was also successfully directed against the International Labor Office, a UN body based in Geneva, whose main official mission was to work for the improvement of working conditions and labor union organizations around the world. As a result of the Communist efforts, the ILO became increasingly political, frequently criticizing labor conditions in the U.S. and other democracies, refusing to investigate charges of labor repression in the Soviet Union, and engaging in non-labor related issues. In 1975 when the ILO voted to admit the Palestine Liberation Organization as official observers during a heated debate in which the U.S. and Israel were viciously attacked, the American delegation walked out for the first time. A few minutes later, the PLO delegation walked in to the cheers of most of the assembly. The PLO leader, Abdel Aziz al-Wajeh, made an opening speech. He was later identified as having directed the PLO massacre of the 11 Israeli athletes at the Olympic Games as well as the terrorist attack on the Hotel Savoy in Tel Aviv, in which 11 guests were killed.

Later in that year, the Ford Administration gave the required two-year notice that the U.S. would withdraw from the ILO if it did not reduce its political activities. In 1977, when there was no sign of improvement, the Carter Administration formally withdrew, depriving the ILO of 25% of its budget.

In 1980, the ILO Director General promised in writing to try to prevent politically motivated resolutions, and the organization showed evidence of not following a double standard when the Soviet Union and other Communist countries were challenged for practices harmful to workers. In February 1980, the U.S. resumed membership.

But the Communist offensive against free labor unions continued in this country and abroad. Typical of the propaganda campaign was the actions of *Counter Spy* Magazine in 1979. This journal had been started by the "Fifth Estate" organization in 1975, with the backing of the Institute for Policy Studies and the advice of opponents of American intelligence like CIA defector Philip Agee, Victor Marchetti, David Dellinger (one of the Chicago Seven), and Mark Lane (attorney for Jim Jones' church, and James Earl Ray).

During 1976, after an internal fight over policy, most of the staff resigned and the magazine stopped publication. Agee and others in 1979, started a new magazine, *Covert Action Information Bulletin,* while *Counter Spy* resumed publication under a new editor, John Kelly. The first issue of the new *Counter Spy* was devoted almost entirely to an attack on the so-called involvement of the CIA in the efforts of AID and the AFL-CIO to assist labor unions in other countries. Following the practice of the old *Counter Spy* in "naming names," this issue listed more than 50 labor union officials from other countries who had simply visited the U.S. Kelly later admitted that there was no evidence that any of these persons were CIA agents, but the magazine used the mere fact that they had visited this country to besmirch their reputations and imply they were tools of American monopolies or the CIA.

Another example was the three-part Public Broadcasting Service television series of the CIA, aired in May 1980, entitled *On Company Business.* Billed as a scholarly documentary, this series produced by Allan Francovich and Howard Drach in fact was a highly prejudiced hatchet job on the CIA. In a fund-raising prospectus circulated in 1976, the producers made clear that their purpose was anything but a balanced investigation: "This film will be the story of 30 years of CIA subversion, murder, bribery and torture as told by an insider . . . it will show the broken lives, hatred, cruelty, cynicism, and despair which result from U.S.-CIA policy." The "insider" was Philip Agee, and many of the other "experts" interviewed on the film were Agee's friends and associates, including Angela Seixas, the Brazilian woman who lived with Agee for several years in England; A.J. Langguth, who wrote the highly distorted book on the Mitrione case, *Hidden Terrors;* and John Stockwell, another CIA defector, who wrote *In Search of Enemies,* a biased account of CIA attempts to counter the Communist conquest of Angola.

The second installment of this series was almost entirely devoted to an attack on American efforts to assist free labor unions in other countries and on efforts to resist Communist subversion of the labor movement. Statements by officials of the AFL-CIO international labor institutes are taken out of context or followed by statements by Agee and his friends making these American efforts appear to be nothing but cynical attempts to use foreign labor unions as tools of U.S. imperialism. The CIA is pictured as using foreign labor unions simply as a means of subverting legally elected foreign governments.

This PBS series was so biased and distorted that it aroused considerable indignation, with many persons questioning the use of the taxpayer-funded broadcasting system to sponsor so prejudiced an attack on American institutions. Communist propaganda had found its way into the heart of a news medium which should belong to the American people. But as the Polish unions illustrate, free labor unions and Communist tyranny cannot coexist, so the propaganda machine cranks up with all its power subtlety against these unions, as we saw in Viet Nam and as we are now seeing in Poland. We can only hope that—as the Reagan victory suggests and as media coverage of Poland may indicate—we are finally beginning to see the reality behind the propaganda.

Just how diametrically opposed are free labor

unions and the Communist system is dramatically indicated by a speech buried in the *On Campus Business* series itself. The producers quoted the speech out of context, intending it to be heard as support for their anti-CIA, anti-AFL-CIO, and anti-Americans stance, but if we remove it from the false context of the television series, it provides a vivid illustration of the graphic contrast between free labor and the Communist world.

Bill Doherty, director of the AFL-CIO's American Institute for Free Labor Development, gave the speech at a luncheon concluding a one-month training session for Latin American labor union officials: Concluding our luncheon today . . . I'd like to give you a thought in Spanish that comes from one of the great political and literary geniuses of this century and of the past century, the true liberator of his country, who is embarrassed from heaven by the shame that now exists in Cuba because of the dictatorship of Fidel Castro. That great Cuban, José Martí, once said:

" 'El mundo se divide en dos ramos: los que aman y construyen, y los que odian y destruyen.' Nosotros compañeros sindicalistas libres, somos que amanos y construimos. Váyanse con Dios, compañeros.''

(" 'The world is divided into two groups: those who love and build, and those who hate and destroy.' Our comrades in free labor unions are those who love and build. Go forth with God, comrades.'')

Communist propaganda has been tragically effective in attacking those who love and build and in supporting those who hate and destroy.

# VIII. Blowing Up The Neutron Bomb*

The Communist campaign against the neutron bomb** has been one of the most massive of all Soviet propaganda efforts and one of the most successful. It has confused the media and public opinion, altered U.S. defense policy to our disadvantage, and blackened the reputation of the American government in the Third World and even in the eyes of our own people.

The neutron bomb story starts in the late 1950s, when American scientists at the Livermore Laboratories developed the concept of a precision atomic weapon with reduced blast and heat effects, but with greater radiation of neutrons. This device could be used to kill enemy soldiers and would greatly reduce

*Written in cooperation with Charles Wiley, Executive Director of the National Committee for Responsible Patriotism.
**"Neutron bomb" is not an accurate description. The present device is not a bomb, but is designed for use in a rocket missile or artillery shell. It is more accurately an "enhanced radiation reduced blast" weapon. Since "neutron bomb" has been so widely adopted by the media, it will be used throughout this chapter.

civilian casualties and destruction of homes and other property in the battle zone.

Such a weapon has great advantages for certain situations. Most of all, it is particularly effective against the major threat to NATO countries: the awesome strength of Soviet tanks and armored personnel carriers massed in Eastern Europe, which by 1975, outnumbered NATO vehicles almost two to one. Defending against this onslaught by conventional atomic weapons would cause massive damage to West Germany and other democracies. Many doubt the West would dare to use tactical atomic bombs—and that doubt, in Soviet minds, could encourage the Communists to risk an invasion.

As soon as the possibility of developing this device was mentioned in the scientific press, the Soviets recognized its importance as a defensive weapon for Western Europe and started a propaganda campaign against it. The first big blast came from Premier Nikita Khrushchev in a speech at a Soviet-Rumanian "Friendship Meeting" on August 11, 1961. "The neutron bomb as conceived by American scientists," he said, "should kill everything living but leave material assets intact. They are acting as robbers who want to murder a man without staining his suit with blood so as to be able to use this suit."

Later the same month, the Russians exploded their bombshell. They resumed atomic bomb testing—a stunning violation of the agreements made three years earlier with the U.S. and other democracies. This was one of the greatest blows to the hopes of mankind ever perpetrated by the Soviet Union, and the Kremlin required a large-scale propaganda effort to contain the public relations problem. They seized on the neutron bomb development in the U.S. as one excuse for resuming the tests.

After the initial shock, President Kennedy and his cabinet decided to defer a decision to resume American tests, and to sit back and await a ground-swell of popular protests around the world and reap to the full the propaganda value of the Soviets' moratorium violation. But *almost nothing happened.* The Kennedy administration, after seven months, reluctantly announced that we were obliged to resume our own testing. *Only then was there an enormous outpouring of demonstrations and denunciations around the world.* Even within the United States there were more organized attacks on Kennedy's decision than had ever been directed against the Russians' initial violation. Women Strike for Peace was formed in September 1961, specifically to put pressure on Kennedy against resuming tests, and the organization mounted vigorous protests after his decision was announced. In subsequent appearances before the House Un-American Activities Committee, ten out of the twelve top officers of W.S.P. took the Fifth Amendment when asked about Communist Party membership. And throughout 1961 and in later years, they agitated continually against American tests and never against Soviet actions.

The bomb was put on the back burner for several years by the Defense Department, but in 1975, Defense Secretary Schlesinger decided to begin production in view of the increasingly serious preponderance of Soviet tank forces in Europe. Soon after this decision was made public in 1977, a major propaganda campaign began, starting in the U.S. and continuing around the world. Organizations like Women Strike for Peace demonstrated in front of the White House using slogans that were notable for being identical to those used by Khrushchev 15 years earlier: 1) a "killer" weapon that destroys people; 2) produces death by radiation which is somehow more horrible than death from other weapons; 3) an "imperialist" bomb, designed to preserve material things. By 1977, the Soviets had a fourth point: this new weapon would "lower the nuclear threshold," making atomic war more likely and threatening detente. In 1977 and '78, these points would be echoed by the media and signs carried by innocent demonstrators who thought their slogans were their own ideas.

In fact, none of these four statements is accurate. In relation to the amount of damage to enemy armed forces, the neutron bomb would actually *save* millions of lives. *All* bombs kill people. This is the tragic reality of war. Neutron bombs do not kill more people per pound of material used than do conventional atomic weapons. They simply have the special advantage that they can kill the same number of combatants with a lesser degree of damage to surrounding homes and property. Since the purpose of most weapons is to kill soldiers, it is illogical to criticize a weapon that can accomplish this with less destruction of civilian establishments.

Such a consideration is especially important in Western Europe, where the potential war theatre is the heavily populated areas of Germany, France and the Low Countries. When we are talking about preserving material things, we are referring not only to factories and other "capitalist" property, but also to homes, churches, hospitals, museums, schools, universities, and all the other treasures of centuries of European history.

Finally, most military analysts agree that the neutron bomb would not lower the nuclear threshold, but would provide a more effective deterrent to Soviet aggression and thus make nuclear war *less* likely.

In June 1977, the campaign against the bomb broke full-scale into the open with a series of articles by Walter Pincus in the *Washington Post*. The series echoed all of the original Communist propaganda points: "killer warhead," "kills people but preserves buildings," etc. After the articles continued for almost three weeks, some under two-column heads on the front page, the *Post* climaxed the series on June 26 with a lead editorial opposing the bomb. Throughout all the articles, there is only a single mention of the main American objective in developing this weapon: to confront a Soviet tank invasion with a credible deterrent that would minimize the destruction of lives, homes and the cultural heritage of the NATO countries. Pincus passed along all the Communist propaganda lines, but not the true aims of the U.S. The Pincus articles were immediately followed by a massive Communist propaganda campaign. Within two days, the Pincus articles were being quoted extensively by *Tass* and *Pravda* and from July 25-August 14, Radio Moscow comments on the bomb received more attention than any other topic. Using this barrage as a kick-off, the Soviets carried the campaign world-wide through other organizations. In July, 1977, the World Peace Council launched a massive campaign against the bomb. Communists organized meetings and demonstrations world-wide during a "Week of Action." Communist China did not join in, letting it be known through several American visitors, that they were heartily in favor of U.S. deployment of the bomb. The campaign reached a climax in February and March 1978 with three international conferences, organized by the W.P.C. The U.S. campaign was led by a constellation of "citizens" groups and think tanks which habitually agitate for unilateral U.S. disarmament and have close ties to the W.P.C. and other Communist fronts.

All this activity had an impact on American news media. Leftist magazines, such as *The Nation* and *The Progressive,* attacked the bomb, parroting the Communist slogans. The TV networks carried both sides of the controversy for a few weeks, then let the subject die. The *NY Times* took a neutral stance but columnist Russell Baker ran one column, "Son of H bomb", an attack based on the threshold argument. *Newsweek,* under the same ownership as the *Washington Post,* launched its coverage with a piece repeating most of the Pincus arguments against the bomb. *Time* gave a balanced presentation, explaining the value of the bomb in defending Western Europe.

In April 1978, Carter, against the advice of many of his advisors, decided to defer the production of the weapon. The main force behind the decision was the furor in the media and the public, stirred up by the propaganda campaign in the U.S. and abroad. The decision caused confusion and alarm in the NATO countries which had been counting on the defense the neutron bomb would provide. By October, 1978, in reaction to grave warnings from the NATO allies, Carter apparently decided that no reciprocal Soviet concessions were forthcoming. Instead, the Russian build-up continued. So he quietly announced the start of production of neutron warhead "parts," which could be assembled in Europe if needed.

The campaign, illustrating the power of the Communist apparatus to mount a tremendous world-wide propaganda effort on command, succeeded in blackening America's reputation in the eyes of millions throughout the world and giving the Soviets an excuse for its mammoth arms build-up. But the Soviets have little need for military weapons when they can win their battles against the unsuspecting West so easily with words alone.

# IX. The Hidden War Against the CIA

The scope and ferocity of the Communist campaign against the CIA are vastly more intense than the campaigns described in previous chapters. Other campaigns have been designed to blunt or cripple American agencies such as AID or policies such as neutron bomb deployment or our assistance to the Cambodian Republic, but the propaganda campaign against the CIA has had the aim of actually *destroying* the agency. This is because the CIA's mission—countering the Communist offensive around the world—brings it into more direct confrontation with the Soviets than any other agency. If the United States is the Soviet Union's main enemy, "glavny vrag," then the CIA is the eyes and ears of this enemy, the bull's-eye at the center of the target. So the Communist war against the CIA has been the longest, fiercest, and most subtle of all.

It is tragic that many of the Western journalists, scholars, and legislators who participated in the blinding and deafening of our eyes and ears—the dismantling of the CIA—did not even realize they were acting as unwitting dupes of the KGB in this war and would never have participated if they had known what was going on. As the propaganda campaign began to succeed in the media and Congress, virtually no one in the media, in Congress, or in the executive branch mentioned that the KGB and its Soviet propaganda organs were promoting attacks on the CIA. Perhaps the greatest irony of all is that even many top CIA officers appeared unaware that Soviet puppeteers were pulling the American strings. Men like William Colby, CIA director during the worst period, seemed blind to the fact of Soviet stimulation of the campaign and made surprising blunders in dealing with the media, blunders which substantially furthered the Soviet effort.

The history of the war against the CIA provides the clearest example of a campaign that started with direct Communist propaganda output and gradually shifted over the years until most of it was coming from American sources. Moscow set the overall objective: destroy the CIA. But more and more tactical planning and implementation came to be carried out by U.S. citizens—Communists, sympathizers and ultra-liberals (many unaware of the Communist inspiration) who were mainly responsible for uncovering the most damaging areas where the CIA could be investigated by journalists or Congress. The Soviets could then follow their usual practice of playing back such American sources in broadcasts from Radio Moscow, in print media and in other vehicles around the world, thus further blackening the reputation of the CIA and American foreign policy.

By the mid-1960s more of the propaganda effort was beginning to come from American sources rather than directly from the Soviet media. The atmosphere in the U.S. was becoming increasingly radical and thus receptive to such agitation, with the country experiencing growing controversy over the Viet Nam War. Communist propaganda against our participation and American mistakes prolonging the war combined to create a heated climate favorable for attacks on many American institutions and the establishment in general. The CIA became a prime target along with the FBI and local police intelligence operations, as part of the Soviet objective of putting out the eyes and ears of its primary enemy, its *"glavny vrag."* Though there is little concrete proof of direct Soviet influence on the Americans who led the campaign against the CIA, this chapter presents four mini-case histories of campaigns that can now be seen to have been based so much on falsehoods or distortions that they must have been the result of either pro-Communist inspirations or manipulation. After years of attack by the Far Left Lobby and the media, CIA director Colby started a policy of being as open as possible with the media and Congress. But the material he released only fueled the arguments of the CIA's enemies.

THE CIA IN CHILE—one of the "affairs" which Colby had a hand in revealing and which ultimately became a mainstay of anti-CIA propaganda starts in 1970 when Salvador Allende-Gossens, a Socialist allied with the Communists, won the Chilean election for the presidency.

Washington was extremely alarmed by the possibility of a second Communist government in the south of Latin America with Castro in the north.

With other crises erupting in other parts of the

world, several last minute and frantic efforts were made to mount some sort of measures via the State Department and the CIA in Chile that might head off an Allende election by the Parliament. The U.S. approached the military on the subject of a coup. But the Chilean Commander in Chief, General Rene Schneider, was reluctant to move. The U.S negotiated with one group of officers who were considering kidnapping General Schneider, removing him to Argentina and launching their own coup. Though the U.S. decided this group was not worthy of support and specifically called off its backing, the group proceeded anyway with the kidnapping attempts. General Schneider resisted and the man was shot. This "assassination" in which the U.S. was in no way involved later figures as one of the major crimes laid at the door of the CIA.

Allende took office and as expected immediately launched a Communist program of nationalization and of attacks on the press, broadcasting and free labor unions. The Communist Party was known to be importing arms, money and foreign agitators to Chile on a large scale, through the Cuban embassy and with Soviet support. On a visit to Santiago, Castro gave strong backing to the new government and warned Allende that he was probably not moving fast enough to control the military. The U.S., through the CIA, provided support to the free forces (non-Communist labor unions, consumer groups, media) to resist Allende's efforts to suppress democracy. Allende's policies were creating inflation and economic chaos and the military at last took action. In September 1973, they overthrew Allende, who was reported to have committed suicide.

The Soviets were furious and launched a major effort to overthrow the new Chilean government and restore a Communist regime. Radio Moscow and Soviet print media claimed that the CIA was responsible for Allende's overthrow. The campaign was soon reflected in U.S. media. Seymour Hersh reported on the subject in the *NY Times.* Congressman Michael Harrington demanded a probe of the CIA's role and the House Intelligence Subcommittee called on Colby to testify. Harrington leaked the contents of Colby's testimony to the *Times,* claiming Colby said the CIA was attempting to "destabilize" the Allende government. Colby denied this, saying that the CIA's mission was only to help democratic elements in Chile survive. But the word "destabilize" became a buzzword in future media and leftist attacks on the CIA, which was accused of "destabilizing legally elected governments" in small countries around the world.

The Chile story became one of the major issues blackening the reputation of the CIA and leading to later congressional investigations and the emasculation of the agency. Like so many of the other attacks on the CIA it was based almost entirely on exaggerations and falsehoods with just enough kernal of truth to be believable to those who wished to think ill of our intelligence services.

The campaign had considerable impact on the media. The allegations against the CIA began to be covered heavily in the *Times* with Seymour Hersh's series, Harrington's leak, and similar articles in the

*Washington Post*. To a large extent, the major television networks are "edited" by the *New York Times* and the *Washington Post*, meaning that the directors of the network news operations turn to these supposed national "newspapers of record" to determine which stories are worth including in the evening news. Too frequently, the network news attitude is that if a story hasn't made the *Times* front page, it's not worth covering (and vice versa). And this surprising dependence of our media on a very few opinion leaders is one of the reasons the Soviets have been so successful with their propaganda campaigns. Once the *Times* and the *Post* decided the CIA in Chile was an important story, the networks followed suit.

An analysis of TV evening news performance during 1974, shows that out of 812 evening news programs, there were 92 items on U.S. and foreign intelligence activity. *The leading topic was CIA activities in Chile*. And like the print media coverage, there was virtually no mention of the activities of the KGB or other Communist subversion in Chile or elsewhere. Out of a total of 168 minutes devoted to intelligence matters, only 4% was devoted to the KGB or other foreign espionage. Like the Far Left Lobby, the networks ignored the CIA's opponent, picturing the CIA as if it were shadowboxing against a non-existent enemy.

DOMESTIC SPYING—our second mini-case history provides an even clearer case of successful Communist manipulation of some of our leading media. The case starts with a December 1974 newspaper article that created a quantum increase in the heat of the war against the CIA. In *Honorable Men*, his memoirs, William Colby offers his version of how the episode began. He says he had a phone call December 18 from Seymour Hersh, who claimed to have a story "bigger than My Lai" about CIA illegal domestic activities. Colby says he was justified in trusting Hersh because a year earlier when he asked Hersh to refrain from writing anything he learned about the Glomar Explorer project, Hersh "honored his request." So he trusted "Sy" to use his discretion in the present investigation and talked to him at some length, assuring Hersh that his information was only scattered exceptional misdeeds and activities that had been subsequently halted.

Colby was not aware that Hersh's earlier silence on the Glomar Explorer had not by any means been patriotic restraint. Hersh had simply not understood then that the project involved recovering a Russian submarine, and he was too busy at the time following up on Watergate to check further.

So Colby was rudely shocked by Hersh's reactions to his interview. As he says sadly, "Hersh did not see it my way at all."

On Sunday, December 22, the *Times* exploded a front page Hersh story, with pictures of Colby, Helms, and Schlesinger and a three column headline:

"Huge CIA Operation Reported in U.S. Against Antiwar Forces." The lead paragraph stated, "The CIA, directly violating its charter, conducted a massive illegal domestic operation during the Nixon administration against the anti-war movement and other dissident groups in the U.S., according to well-placed Government sources." Colby, naive to the end, had allowed himself to be used as a "well-placed Government source" in the campaign that almost destroyed the agency he was supposed to lead.

This was the final major breaking of the dam of media restraint in publishing any variety of leak, rumor or slander that might be available. For the prestigious *Times* to give the story this sort of play opened the way for other media to join the campaign.

Hersh followed up with several more stories giving additional details. On at least one story, he seems to have been the clear victim of a KGB disinformation agent. On December 29, he reported an elaborate "confession" by a CIA "ex-agent" who claimed to have worked for four years spying on radicals in New York City, not only infiltrating student activist groups but also participating in break-ins, wire-taps, and the use of a "boom microphone" to overhear distant conversations. This, incidentally, was the only story by an actual participant in domestic spying to appear in the *Times*. But no such activities were ever confirmed by later *Times* checking, by the investigations conducted by the Senate and House Intelligence Committees, or by the Rockefeller Commission. And the *Times* was never able to produce the man to testify. Harry Rositzke, a former CIA officer, in his book, *CIA's Secret Operations*, says he was probably a disinformation "walk-in."

When Hersh's story was later the basis for investigations by the Senate and the Rockefeller Commission, it was found to be greatly exaggerated and overblown.

Hersh was nominated for the Pulitzer Prize but failed to get it. The *Times*, however, continued to follow up on the story. By giving such prominent play initially to this story of "massive domestic wrongdoing," the *Times* had maneuvered itself into a position of being committed to CIA misdeeds, so that no matter what the evidence later turned out to be, the *Times*, from Managing Editor Rosenthal on down, was committed to supporting his point of view. In fact, after Hersh failed to get the Pulitzer and his article was criticized for being overblown, the *Times* and many of its columnists and reporters, like Anthony Lewis and James McNaughton seemed to make a special effort to plead the case that Hersh had been right and his story "confirmed."

In any case, the damage had been done. The Hersh story and it followers resulted in:

—consternation in the CIA and the Ford Administration.

—appointment by Ford of a commission under Nelson Rockerfeller to investigate the domestic activities of the CIA.

—Senate establishment of a special committee to investigate the CIA under Senator Church.

—later follow-up in the House with an investigation under Otis Pike.

Colby calls the subsequent year of 1975 "The Year of Intelligence." It was a period when the CIA was hit by torpedoes from every direction. Colby, required to testify two or three or even five times a week during the year before the Rockefeller Commission and the various congressional committees, also had to attempt to maintain some sort of open relations with the media.

He made his first appearance before the Rockefeller Commission on January 13 and the Senate Armed Services and Appropriations Committees on January 15. He presented a frank and open summary of CIA activities with comments that illegal activities were minimal and had been terminated in earlier years. There was a sympathetic reception by both groups, but the Senate insisted on releasing his testimony. The *Times* published a front page Hersh article with two-page summary of Colby remarks, emphasizing misdeeds. Significantly, Colby started his statement with the phrase, "I flatly deny...", but Hersh's lead begins, "Colby admits..." As usual, the *Times* treatment caused another sensation in the country and further furor in Congress and the media.

ASSASSINATIONS—the third mini-case history concerns the furor over CIA assassination attempts and illustrates again the failure of high American officials, from Colby all the way up to President Ford, to appreciate the adversary position of the media on intelligence matters. Ford himself was responsible for the initial leak on assassinations. On January 16, 1975, he hosted a luncheon for Arthur Sulzberger and the top editors of the *New York Times* at the White House. When the subject of the Rockefeller Commission came up, Ford was asked whether its make-up of "conservative and establishment" figures did not detract from its credibility. He replied that he needed reliable men on the panel to insure that it did not delve into secrets that might "blacken the reputation of every U.S. president since Truman." "Like what?" asked *Times* Managing Editor Abe Rosenthal. "Like assassinations," said Ford, and then, realizing what he had said, he added, "That's off the record!"

Of course this remark leaked within two weeks and became a common topic of conversation in media circles. Daniel Schorr learned of it just shortly before an interview he had obtained with William Colby on February 27. He raised the subject towards the end of the interview in an off-hand way. Since the Rockefeller Commission's charter covered only activities within the U.S., he asked Colby whether the CIA had ever assassinated any one in this country. Colby was startled that Ford had mentioned such a topic and replied simply, "Not in this country." Schorr, startled, in turn realized that this meant the CIA had committed or at least attempted assassinations abroad. He asked Colby "Who?" but Colby refused to answer any further questions. Schorr now thought he had a sensational story, which he proceeded to broadcast on CBS the following evening, that "President Ford has repeatedly warned associates that if current investigations go too far they could uncover several assassinations of foreign officials involving the CIA."

For nine months, the subject of assassinations became another major subject of frequent headlines and sensational broadcasts, spearheaded by almost daily pronouncements by Daniel Schorr on CBS and leading to further blackening of the reputation of the CIA and the American government. The administration was obliged to widen the mandate of the Rockefeller Commission to include assassinations, and the subject was added to the topics to be investigated by the Church Committee of the Senate. The investigations were secret, but they led to endless leaks and attempts of the media to catch witnesses before or after testimony.

The Church Committee issued its report on assassinations in November 1975. The Committee concluded that the CIA had been "involved" in plots against five foreign leaders. But a careful reading of its report shows that the Agency, in fact, made efforts to assassinate only two of these: Castro and Lumumba, both unsuccessful. (See Chart II on following page.)

The assassination story is another case where all of the propaganda impetus came from American sources, wittingly or unwittingly following the Communist objective of attacking the CIA with the purpose of destroying it. The details were picked up by Soviet media and played back all around the world. Communist propaganda in Latin America, Africa, India and elsewhere made frequent reference to "CIA Assassination Teams" to cast doubt on American diplomatic efforts in those areas.

THE GLOMAR EXPLORER—This fourth mini-case history of another campaign that damaged the CIA and in fact, American security in general, had its origin back in 1968. In February, of that year, a Soviet "G Class" missile submarine left her pen in Vladivostok and sailed out into the Pacific. Somewhere in the mid-Pacific, she met disaster due to a malfunction which led to a series of explosions, rupturing her plates and causing her to sink out of control and at increasing speed until she hit bottom more than three miles deep.

The U.S. Navy network of underwater monitoring devices tracking her progress detected the disaster and made a horrifying recording of the actual sounds of the fatal descent with fracturing plates and bodies and other objects slamming into steel bulkheads audible on the tape. The Navy was thus in possession of an exact fix on a wrecked Soviet submarine, and it realized that the Soviets were unaware of the accident and had no knowledge of the sub's location. Naval officials decided that the recovery of a Soviet submarine would yield priceless knowledge of Russian naval architecture, missile techniques, nuclear weaponry, code books and other data. The CIA and the Navy contracted with Howard Hughes' Summa Corporation and Global Marine, Inc., to build the Glomar Explorer, under a cover story that it was to be used to mine mineral nodules from the ocean floor. The salvage operation was carried out in the Pacific in the summer of 1974. The CIA said only about half the sub was brought to the surface and they planned to recover the rest in 1975. Other reports say the entire sub was recovered, perhaps in three pieces. Most knowledgeable comments say the information gained on Soviet technology and codes was worth far more than the several hundred million dollar cost of the project.

Security was tight, but a few journalists, including Seymour Hersh, found out early in 1974 that the Glomar Explorer was preparing some important project, without learning its true purpose. Colby persuaded them to drop the story because of its importance to national security. However, in 1975, Hersh re-entered the case. In his book, *On Press*, Tom Wicker says Hersh attacked the story with his usual "ferocity," flew to the West Coast, and within a week had a "complete" story, which Hersh said was worth six columns in the *Times*. Colby appealed to the *Times* management and Sulzberger and Rosenthal agreed to hold up the story until Colby said it was no longer crucial or until another medium broke it. That break came when Charles Morgan, Jr. head of the Washington office of the ACLU, and active in the Far Left Lobby, learned that the Glomar Explorer was involved in some secret work more important than its cover story. He called Jack Anderson, the columnist, to alert him to the story. Les Whitten, Anderson's assistant, called Hersh, and Hersh, according to Wicker, gave Whitten "suggestions of further sources." Whitten called Hersh back to say that Anderson had enough information to break the story and would broadcast it that night, March 18, 1975.

The media enlarged on the Glomar incident for several months, some even implying it was an attempt to create good publicity for the CIA, that there had been no real effort to recover the sub, and that it had been a waste of money, with Colby's efforts to maintain a security ploy to cover up CIA waste. It isn't clear from reports available whether the CIA did in fact plan to go back the following summer or whether this was a cover story used by Colby to persuade the media to hold off, to hide the recovery of the sub from the Soviets. In either case, the Morgan-Anderson-Hersh combination, by blowing the project, gravely injured a major valuable enterprise by the CIA and did considerable harm to national security.

During 1975, the Far Left Lobby and the media continued a barrage of attacks on the CIA, exploiting the CIA's drug experiments, the development of a poison dart gun (Colby himself revealed this weapon in a televised open hearing of the Senate Committee) and the use of a harmless chemical that had been sprayed in the NY subway system by the Army several years earlier to determine whether an enemy could saturate the subways with poison. Colby says the CIA, in 1975, was required to report on such activities as the Mayaguez incident off Cambodia and other covert operations to no less than eight Congressional committees and every one of the operations leaked. Colby was fired by President Ford on November 2, 1975, probably for his excessive openness.

In January 1976, the House Committee completed its report on the CIA and voted to keep the report confidential. However, a copy of the report was given, under the table, to CBS reporter Daniel Schorr, who citing his "journalistic duty" published major portions of the report in the *Village Voice's* February 16, 1976 issue, with a front page headline: "The Report of the CIA That President Ford Doesn't Want You to Read."

This leak provoked another uproar in the country and the House of Representatives, but this time in the form of some backlash against the continuing leaks and harassment of the CIA. Schorr was subpoened by the House Committee and there was a move to have him declared in contempt. But the House was unable to discover the source of the leak and Schorr refused to name it, invoking freedom of the press. The House Committee voted not to hold him in contempt. But Schorr was discharged by CBS.

One of the most important conclusions of the House report was an apparent dig at the Church Committee, who claimed the CIA had been a "rogue elephant out of control." Evidence suggests that the CIA, far from being out of control, had been utterly responsive to the instructions of the American Presidents.

The report, however, was critical of the CIA, describing failures to predict crises in Viet Nam (the Tet offensive), Cyprus and India, coups in Portugal, the Mid East War and the 1968 Soviet invasion of Czechoslovakia. The CIA called the report "biased, perjorative and inaccurate." The Senate Intelligence Committee's report (April 1976) also rejected the notion that the CIA was "out of control" and said that American agencies "have made important contributions to the nation's security, and generally performed their missions with dedication and distinction." While highly critical of CIA actions in the domestic field, the facts as presented in the report did not add up to a serious indictment. Nevertheless, the *Times* and other media played up the report as further documentation of CIA crimes and the findings were widely reported by Soviet media with critical comments, mainly from American sources.

When Carter took office in 1977, the war on the CIA was widened. In order to unify the Democratic Party, he made many concessions to the McGovern wing and their sympathizers, appointing large numbers of ultra-liberal and radical followers of this group to the new administration. Under the guidance of such officials, a further dismantling of the CIA took place, with firings of over 800 people. Counter intelligence virtually went out of business and covert intelligence, said one veteran, lost the equivalent of thousands of years of experience. The Administration further restricted the activities of the CIA, limiting its power of surveillance and its ability to gather covert information and counter-intelligence. Meanwhile, Congress and the Administration were struggling to devise a "Charter" that would formalize the new regulations for the CIA and the intelligence community. But by late 1978, Carter, who had earlier decried "the inordinate fear of Communism" was becoming alarmed at the breakdown of our intelligence capability. Between

1978 and 1980, the Carter administration experienced several intelligence disasters, including the excesses of the Khomeni regime in Iran and the seizure of the hostages, and the Soviet invasion of Afghanistan. Carter said that his ideas on Soviet aims had changed more in the two weeks following this invasion than in his entire previous career. In the spring of 1980, Carter was demanding a stronger intelligence capability, and Congress abandoned efforts to write a new charter for the CIA. In effect, American intelligence was going to be allowed to rebuild some of its own strength with a congressional policy of looking the other way. The *Times* wrote an indignant editorial on the abandonment of the charter and Tom Wicker and other ultraliberal journalists wrote similar blasts.

The one-sided offensive by the media and Far Left Lobby and the hemorrhaging of classified information did immeasurable harm to the morale of the CIA, possibilities of recruiting foreign agents in the future, relations with allied foreign intelligence operations and CIA operations in general. The propaganda also succeeded in causing over-reaction by Congress and the administration, probably going beyond the opinions of the American public. The campaign started by the Kremlin and carried forward later by sympathizers and agents in the U.S. succeeded in almost crippling the CIA. Up until the middle of 1980, the Soviets appeared to be close to their goal of total destruction. But by that time, a popular reaction had set in and even President Carter was having second thoughts. The 1980 election reflected this backlash even more clearly. The current administration and Senate majority, working with like-minded representatives in the House, have an enormous task to restore the CIA to its former effectiveness. Perhaps the most frightening lesson of all has to do with the ease with which our media has been manipulated. The KGB and its propaganda apparatus have learned to get our "free press" to do their work for them in destroying the eyes and ears of the USSR's main enemy, "glavny vrag."

# CHART II

## FACTS VS. ALLEGATIONS ON ASSASSINATION ATTEMPTS

| Leader | Facts | Comments |
|---|---|---|
| Castro | Several attempts, all unsuccessful. | Weight of evidence shows CIA launched attempts only on orders from very high authority, most probably with knowledge of Kennedys. Should be judged in light of conditions at that time. Castro was first breach in containment policy, a Communist dictatorship within 90 miles of U.S. During period of these attempts he was allowing Soviets to prepare to install nuclear missiles, a major threat to U.S., leading to "Missile Crisis." He was later quoted as criticizing Soviets for backing down and withdrawing missiles. |
| Lumumba | In 1960 CIA officers were ordered to devise plot to assassinate Lumumba, evidently with knowledge of Eisenhower and Allen Dulles. Attempt never materialized and Lumumba was later shot by Congolese rivals, with no CIA involvement. | |
| Trujillo | U.S. cooperated with dissidents in Dominican Republic. Supplied them with arms, but had no direct involvement in assassination. | Trujillo was one of the most brutal dictators in Latin American history. CIA and U.S. government cannot be criticized for encouraging his overthrow. |
| Diem | U.S. Government and CIA were privy to plot by South Vietnamese military to overthrow Diem, and gave it cautious support, but did not cooperate with or approve of assassination. | Assassination was evidently unauthorized even by the South Vietnamese coup leaders, but was carried out by junior officers. U.S. not involved. |
| General Schneider (Chile) | Killed by plotters who had been in contact with CIA. But CIA had specifically disapproved assassination and no U.S. weapons were used. | |

115

# X.  Balance Sheet

The Balance Sheet method, in which an individual's output—publications, public statements, etc.—is used here as an approach to measuring the degree of Communist propaganda influence on some prominent figures in the media. If the Debits, statements in harmony with the Communist line, heavily outweigh the Credits, statements opposed to the Communist Line, this is persuasive evidence that the individual, if not an agent, is at least being strongly influenced by Communist propaganda, consciously or unconsciously, or has views closely approximating it. In many cases, the Debits are based partially on the truth. But if the individual in question has written only about such "truths" and never about the anti-Communist truths, he is as suspect as those whose output consists totally of falsehoods.

The following are balance sheets on four individuals and two organizations that have been influential in the events described in this book.

## Seymour Hersh

Graduate, University of Chicago. Joined AP in Washington, 1965. Washington Bureau of the *New York Times* in 1972.

DEBITS:

1967—Articles on U.S. chemical and biological warfare in *New Republic*:

"Just a Drop Can Kill," May 6.

"Germs and Gas as Weapons," June 7

"Gas and Germ Warfare," July 1

"But Don't Tell Anyone I Told You," December 9.

1968—*Chemical and Biological Warfare: America's Hidden Arsenal* (Doubleday). Publisher later claimed this was major influence in U.S. decision to halt production of these weapons. (It is now apparent that the Soviets continued to produce these weapons in violation of the Biological Warfare Convention signed with the U.S. in 1975 outlawing their use.)

—Press Secretary to Senator Eugene McCarthy for his presidential campaign, during which McCarthy opposed the U.S. effort in Viet Nam and recommended lower defense spending. Hersh resigned from McCarthy's staff after campaign and criticized McCarthy for being "nothing but a liberal." with no feeling for "the revolution."

1969—Article, "On Uncovering the Great Gas Cover-up," *Ramparts*, June. (Here he is already using phrase, "cover-up.")

—Begins an investigation of Lt. Calley and the My
Lai incident. (Indications that the Communists
facing a major propaganda problem over the
massacre of 2,000 leading Hue citizens by the
North Vietnamese, saw the My Lai affair as a
possible distraction.) The Stern Foundation
and Stern's Foundation for Investigative Journalism, headed by James Boyd, backed Hersh's
investigation and arranged for the almost mori-
bund Dispatch News Service to distribute
Hersh's stories. The My Lai industry was
launched and the Hue massacre virtually ignored by the media.

—*My Lai*, published by Random House.

—Institute for Policy Studies publishes *The Pentagon Watchers: Student Reports on the National Security State*, a book based on summer
work by students under the guidance of Hersh,
NACLA, and others.

—Joins Advisory Board of Fund for Investigative
Journalism.

1972—*Cover Up*, on My Lai (Random House).

1973—Front page *NY Times* article on U.S. "secret"
air raids against Cambodian sanctuaries in
1970.

1974—*Times* articles leaking Congressional testimony
on CIA's activities in Chile before Allende's
overthrow.

—Front page *Times* article on CIA's "massive illegal spying," December 22. Followed up by al-

most daily articles containing highly exaggerated, often inaccurate information. Hersh nominated, but failed to get Pulitzer prize because articles considered overblown and poorly researched.

1975—*Glomar Explorer*, secret to recover sunken Russian submarine in Pacific, blown by Hersh, Jack Anderson, and Charles Morgan of ACLU.

1977—*Times* favorable review of Arthur Sampson's *The Arms Race*, which blames the West for creating the race, but does not mention the Communist build-up causing the race.

1978—Front page *Times* story on CIA recruitment of blacks in the '60s to infiltrate Black Panthers and other radical groups in U.S. and abroad.

—*Times* story on John Stockwell's book, *In Search of Enemies*, attacking CIA's Angola policies.

—Article in *Times* on lapses in monitoring of CIA's covert actions by Congressional Oversight Committees. (Representative Edward P. Boland, Chairman of House Committee on Intelligence, writes in an issue the following week to say that Hersh article is misleading.)

—Front page *Times* article on leaked Senate Intelligence Committee report saying that Colby and Kissinger misled Congress on U.S. role in Angola. Colby and Kissinger deny charges.

1979—*Times* article says CIA rejected warning on Shah.

—In August, Hersh is one of few American journalists to be allowed to visit Viet Nam. During and after a 10 day visit, he writes a series of six articles for the *Times*, which generally pass along the North Vietnamese propaganda line, including:

After six hours of interviews with Vietnamese Foreign Minister, Hersh quotes him as blaming U.S. for failure to "normalize" relations with Viet Nam.

There has been no bloodbath.

The "reeducation camps" are austere, but there is no starvation or cruelty.

Refugees are simply those who had cooperated with the Americans, became used to the easy life with American assistance, and could not get accustomed to austere life under Communism.

The Government is not extracting money from the refugees.

Horrors exist in Cambodia. (Now a major theme in Vietnamese propaganda to stress the horrors of the Pol Pot regime and thus justify the Vietnamese conquest of Cambodia.)

The Soviets are not seeking military bases in Viet Nam. (Actually, intelligence is now overwhelming that the Soviet Navy is making use of Cam Rahn Bay and Danang Harbor, although the Russians may not have set up their own "bases" there.)

The New Economic Zones have been having some minor problems, but in general, the people are content there. (By coincidence, one of the same issues of the *Times* carrying the

Hersh story from Viet Nam, also ran a short news item with directly contradictory evidence.)

There is a relatively free press. One of Hersh's six articles is entirely devoted to an interview with a newspaper editor in Ho Chi Minh City (formerly Saigon), who said he is able to publish almost anything he pleases with only mild "guidance" from the government. Hersh must be incredibly naive—or something worse—to accept this propaganda as truth.

1980—Op Ed *Times* on Iran mission says, "Perhaps the failure of the operation will be as instructive for Jimmy Carter as was the Bay of Pigs for John F. Kennedy in 1961." In other words, the advice of the Intelligence and military communities cannot be trusted.

CREDITS:

No articles can be found that could be considered against the Communist line. For example, in all his voluminous writings on My Lai, there is no mention of much greater massacres by the Communists, of which Hue was only one. His 1979 series of articles on his Viet Nam visit contains nothing about the reported horrors in the reeducation centers, the suppression of free press and free religion, the Americans missing in action, growing Soviet influence, and other problems. He has produced no articles on the activities on the KGB, which represent a vastly greater threat to American liberties than his favorite target, the CIA. In fact, he has expressed exactly the opposite view, that the KGB represents no threat. At the Accuracy in Media conference in Washington in November of 1979, at the end of a question period, he was asked the following:

*Q: Mr. Hersh, this conference is entitled "The Media and the Present Danger." Do you believe there is a danger, and if so, what is it?*

Hersh: There is no danger. I don't believe it. There is no danger of the KGB penetrating the U.S. to the point where our institutions are at stake. (Laughter) I consider that a James Angleton fantasy. I really do. I think we are in terrific shape.

## Gareth Porter. PhD.

from Cornell. On faculty of Center for International Studies, Cornell, 1964-68. Joined Indochina Resource Center, 1970 (one of leading organizations opposing Viet Nam War).

DEBITS:

1968—"People As the Enemy," *New Republic*. Attack on U.S. policy in Viet Nam.

1969—"Diemist Restoration," *Commonweal*. Attack on South Vietnamese government.

—"Vietnam: The Bloodbath Argument," *Commonweal*. Asserts that South Vietnamese need not fear a Communist takeover and that stories of bloodbath in North Vietnam after their victory there are false.

1971—Correspondent and "bureau chief" in Saigon

for the leftist Dispatch News Service. (See above under Hersh.)

1970-74—Voluminous publications, via Indochina Resource Center, opposing U.S. efforts in Viet Nam, painting North Vietnamese and Viet Cong as patriotic nationalists and urging government of "national reconciliation."

1975—"Pressing Ford to Drop Thieu," *New Republic*.
— "Viet Nam: Reconciliation Begins." *Christian Century.*
— *A Peace Denied: The U.S., Viet Nam, and the Paris Peace Agreement*, Indiana University Press. The thesis of the book states that "the policies of the U.S. were the cause of the war and the major stumbling block preventing a negotiated settlement."

1976—Porter gives principal speech at meeting in Union Theological Seminary welcoming Ieng Sary, Foreign Minister of new Pol Pot Cambodian Communist government, on his arrival in New York for UN session. No mention of reports of massacres by Communists in Cambodia.
— "Viet Nam's Long Road to Socialism," *Current History.* Highly optimistic account of the new Vietnamese government's attempts to build "socialism."
— Actively campaigns against release of Fellowship of Reconciliation letter to Vietnamese government appealing for more human rights and an open society.

1977—Testifies before House Subcommittee on International Relations, says reports of massacres in
Cambodia are false.

—Leaves Indochina Resource Center, joins Institute for Policy Studies, Far Left Lobby group.

—"Healing the Wounds of War; Justice not Peace
for Viet Nam," *Christian Century.*

—"Kissinger's Double Cross for Peace," *Nation*.

1979—Viet Nam invades Cambodia (ignoring UN),
overthrows Pol Pot, and sets up puppet government. In telephone interview with author,
Porter says Vietnamese invasion of Cambodia
is justified.

1980—Joins the Center for International Policy, another organization active in the Far Left Lobby.

CREDITS:

No record of any Porter writings contrary to the
Communist line on Indo-China. Defended the brutal
Pol Pot regime until it became permissable to attack
Cambodia in order to justify Vietnamese invasion. Opposed U.S. policy in Viet Nam, gave steady optimistic
picture of developments, after the fall of Saigon. In
spite of knowledge on Vietnamese affairs, failed to
criticize the tyranny that was evident and tried to suppress others' attempts to do so.

## Morton H. Halperin. PhD.

Harvard. On staff of Harvard Center for International

Affairs, 1960-65.
DEBITS:
1961—An early advocate of unilateral American disarmament.
—A Proposal for a Ban on Nuclear Weapons, suggests that U.S. should disarm even if Soviets do
not and that inspection is "not absolutely nec-
essary."

1966-68—Defense Department, Deputy Asst. Secretary, reports to Leslie H. Gelb, responsible for prepara-
tion of Pentagon Papers, critical of U.S. role in Viet
Nam.

1969—Hired by Kissinger for National Security Council.
—FBI names him as most likely suspect for having leaked story of secret bombing of Cambodian sanctuaries. Kissinger takes him off list of
those allowed to see top secret documents. He
is one of first to have phones tapped by
"Plumbers" operation, designed to curb serious government leaks. (No evidence was
found that he was the leaker.) Later resigns
from National Security Council.

1972—Testimony before House Appropriations Committee, recommends series of drastic progressive cuts in defense expenditure, eliminating
multiple warheads on missiles, Minuteman III,
Trident submarine, and several advanced
fighter planes, and also eliminate two out of
our three legs of the three-legged defense system, i.e. bombers and land-based missiles,

leaving only nuclear subs (the least accurate).

1974—Joins Center for National Security Studies, Far Left think tank.

—"Covert Operations, Effects of Secrecy on Decision-Making," paper presented at Conference on Intelligence, sponsored by CNSS. Recommends removing secret classification from U.S., satellite reconnaisance operations and National Security Agency communications intercepts, and a greatly reduced operations role for CIA.

1975—"Most Secret Agents," *New Republic*.
"Led Astray by the CIA," *New Republic*.
"CIA Denying What's Not in Writing," *New Republic*.
"Activists at the CIA," *New Republic*.

1976—Director of Project on National Security and Civil Liberties, a joint operation of CNSS and ACLU. Concentrating on investigating and reducing role of FBI, CIA, police departments and other internal security organizations.

—Co-author of *The Lawless State: The Crimes of the U.S. Intelligence Agencies*. (Penguin)

—"Did Richard Helms Commit Perjury?" *New Republic*.

—"Public Secrets," *New Republic*.

—Board member of the Committee For Public Justice. Principal organizer was Lillian Hellman, who has never renounced her support of Stalinist Russia. (Other Board members include admitted Communist Jessica Mitford.)

1977—Chairperson, Campaign to Stop Government Spying (founded with backing of National Lawyers Guild). Frequent testimony before Congressional Committees, recommending strict limits on operations of CIA, FBI, and other security organizations.

1978—Testimony before House Committee on Intelligence regarding the Foreign Intelligence Surveillance Act. Recommends no surveillance be permitted unless there is prior evidence of criminal activity (which most experts say would cripple investigative process).
—Becomes Director of CNSS.
—Co-signer of letters to Justice Department, as head of Project on National Security, opposing all wiretaps except with prior evidence of criminal activity.

CREDITS:

No record of any writings or statements against the Communist line. All CNSS "studies" of "national security" have generally attacked the methods of CIA, FBI, and other U.S. security organizations, recommending drastic restrictions. But his organizations have never mentioned the KGB or other Communist subversive activities.

## Saul Landau

MA in History, University of Wisconsin. One of the

most active associates of the Institute for Policy Studies and Director of their subsidiary, the Transnational Institute. Left-wing agitator, film producer, mostly far left propaganda documentaries.

DEBITS:

1959—On Editorial board of *Studies on the Left,* radical magazine.

—Collaborated with C. Wright Mills, writer prominent in Far Left and pro-Castro causes in the 1950s and '60s. Accompanied Mills on trips to Cuba and Europe.

1961—Speaks as a representative of the Fair Play for Cuba Committee at American-Cuban Friendship Rally in New York City, sponsored by Advance, youth organizations of the Communist Party. (The Fair Play for Cuba Committee went out of existence in 1964 when Lee Harvey Oswald was revealed as a member.)

1962—Featured speaker at pro-Castro rally at Berkeley, sponsored by Trotskyite Socialist Workers Party and similar rally at Stanford.

1963—Joins with about 100 leftists in the formation of a new leftist movement, "The San Francisco Opposition," or "The Opposition."

1964—Fired from his hospital social work job for promoting the showing of *Un Chant D'Amour,* a French film about homosexual love and sadism, produced by Jean Genet, the French homosexual and ex-convict. Film co-sponsored by SDS, "The Opposition," and SLATE, a radical student group at Berkeley. (Landau eventually took his case on the banning of the film to court, and in 1966, the California District Court of Appeals handed down a decision saying that the film was nothing less than hardcore pornography and should be banned. *Time* Magazine called the film "a silent 30 minute portrayal of a sadistic prison guard alternately beating and spying on four convicts engaged in homosexual acts." This was Landau's first highly-publicized entrance into film distribution or producing.)

1965—Active in Students for a Democratic Society (SDS) affairs, speaking at benefits, serving as instructor in SDS's "New School" in San Francisco.

—Joins staff of *Ramparts*, radical magazine.

1966—Active in the North American Congress on Latin America (NACLA), new radical organization formed by former SDS members who were becoming too old to be considered "students." Objectives are research and action on "the real forces shaping U.S. policy in Latin America—corporations, government agencies, foundations, churches, and unions."

1967—Attends International Cultural Congress in Havana as a film maker. Landau's wife, Nina Serrano Landau, attends Communist Youth Festival in Moscow and then travels to Red China, in violation of State Department regulations.

1969—Produces two propaganda films about Cuba:

*Report from Cuba* and *Fidel*.

1970—Film, *Que Hacer,* ("What Is to be Done"), on "revolution" in Chile.

—On editorial board of *Socialist Revolution,* new pro-Communist magazine in San Francisco.

1971—Film, *Brazil—A Report on Torture.* Co-producer is Haskell Wexler, radical film maker who accompanied Jane Fonda on one of her trips to North Viet Nam and has produced films for the NLF and other Far Left organizations.

1972—Film, *Robert Wall—Ex-FBI Agent.* "Confessions of a former FBI agent who describes how he spied on the IPS, Stockely Carmichael and others.
—Film, *The Jail,* a trip through the society of "prisoners, jailers, transvestites, murderers, drunks and sadists."
—Film, *An Interview With Allende,* co-produced with Haskell Wexler.

1973—Film, *Song for Dead Warriors,* "examines the reasons for the Wounded Knee occupation in the Spring of 1973 by Oglala Sioux Indians and members of the American Indian Movement."

1975—Film, *Cuba and Fidel,* a "film picture postcard of Cuba with interviews of Fidel on socialist law, the difference between Russians and Americans, and Cuba before and after the Revolution."

1976—Film, *Land of My Birth,* on "Jamaica's charis-
matic Prime Minister, Michael Manley, in the
midst of his election campaign."

—Letelier killed by bomb blast under his car in
Washington along with IPS associate Ronni
Moffitt. Letelier papers found in his brief case
include a letter from Landau to be delivered to
a friend in Cuba, saying, "I think at age 40 the
time has come to dedicate myself to narrower
pursuits, namely making propaganda for American Socialism. . . . we cannot any longer just
help our third world movements and revolution, although obviously we shouldn't turn our
backs on them. . . ." Landau takes over the
publicity on Letelier's killing and the campaign
to get the maximum propaganda value against
the Chilean Government. Later succeeds Letelier as Director of Transnational Institute.

1978—Film, *In Search of Enemies,* with Wexler, based
on Stockwell's book attacking CIA role in Angola.

—Article in *Mother Jones,* radical magazine, partially funded by IPS, "Behind the Letelier Murder," blames the CIA for a part in the killing
because of its encouragement of the Chilean
intelligence organization. No word in here, or
another Landau IPS output on Letelier about
his receiving money from Cuban intelligence.

1980—Book, *Assassination on Embassy Row,* by
John Dinges and Landau, continues propaganda campaign against Chile, CIA, and U.S.

government, based on Letelier killing. Receives a moderately favorable review in New York Times, although reviewer says, "the main actors in the drama are superficially and sometimes clumsily portrayed. . . . We are expected to believe that the first word spoken by Letelier's infant son, Christian, was 'Allende'."

CREDITS:

There is no record of any of Landau's films or published works that could be considered critical of Communist aggression, subversion, or tyranny.

## The Center for National Security Studies

This organization was founded in 1974 through the initiative of the National Lawyers Guild and the Institute for Policy Studies. It was funded initially by the Fund for Peace and the American Civil Liberties Union Foundation. (For further details, see Chapter II.) The following balance sheet of its published works is taken from its "Publications" for March 1980:

DEBITS:

—*The Lawless State: The Crimes of the U.S. Intelligence Agencies* by Halperin, Jerry Berman, Robert Borosage and Christine Marwick. Covers the activities of the CIA, FBI, IRS, military intelligence and "politically motivated" grand juries, and details such operations as the overthrow of the "democratic government" of Chile.

—*The CIA File,* edited by Borosage and John Marks. Papers presented at the 1974 CNSS Conference on the CIA, entirely by CIA opponents, except for William Colby, who was subjected to an hour and a half harangue during the question period.

—*FBI Charter Legislation Comparison.* Compares the proposed FBI Charter Act of 1979 with other recommendations, including Attorney General Levi's guidelines, the Church Committee proposals, and recommendations by opponents of the FBI, like the ACLU and the Committee for Public Justice.

—*The CIA and the Freedom of Information Act: Report on the Proposal for an Exemption.* Criticizes the CIA's testimony that the present FOIA is crippling the Agency's ability to maintain foreign agents and gain cooperation for foreign intelligence services.

—*From Officials' File: Abstracts of Documents on National Security and Civil Liberties Available from CNSS Library.* Catalogue of materials in CNSS files, available for researchers. Documents have been obtained by FOIA releases and discovery processes in law suits, most formerly classified. Many obtained "only after a courtroom struggle." Includes such items as: transcripts of Kissinger's off-the-record press conferences on Middle East and SALT, FBI surveillance of J. Robert Oppenheimer, DOE Report on uranium diversion and theft, documents on intelligence operations by state and local police, etc.

—*Comparison of Proposals for Reforming the Intelligence Communities,* by Berman, Mark Drooks, Halperin, and Barbara Pollack. Compares the Church Committee report, Carter's Executive Order and the Senate Intelligence Committee 1978 and 1980 bills.

—*Nuclear Power and Civil Liberties,* by Allan Adler and Jay Peterzell. "Critics of nuclear power have said it presents a major risk to civil liberties because the nuclear materials provide a powerful justification for surveillance of protestors and other measures."

—*Operation Chaos* by Jay Peterzell, Comparison of Church Committee account of CHAOS with other later information gained through FOIA and lawsuit by ACLU.

—*Freedom vs. National Security* by Halperin and David Hoffman. 600 page "sourcebook" on cases and statutes on such topics as Pentagon Papers, CIA, Viet Nam, and Watergate.

—*The Federal Bureau of Investigation.* A pamphlet that "reviews the Bureau's history and lays out recommendations for reform. . . . The FBI's long-term apparatus for surveilling American citizens and targeting movements for social change have not been put under control."

—*National Security and Civil Liberties* by Morton Halperin. Deals with wiretap law.

—*The CIA Corporate Shell Game* by John Marks. On CIA proprietary companies such as Air America, which "are another area of unregulated clandestine operations."

—*The Grand Juries: An American Inquisition,* by Judy Mead.

—*Top Secret: National Security and the Right to Know,* by Halperin and Hoffman. Case studies of "several of the country's biggest secrecy snafus—the Pentagon Papers, the bombing of Cambodia, the Angolan intervention."

—*Documents: A Collection from the Secret Files of the American Intelligence Community,* by Christy Macy and Susan Kaplan. Reproduces "a selection from the paper trail left behind by improper intelligence agency programs."

—*FOIA Litigation Manual,* edited by Christine Marwick. Technical manual for attorneys on "all aspects of Freedom of Information and Privacy Acts."

—*Using the Freedom of Information Act: A Step by Step Guide.*

CREDITS:

There is no record that the Center for National Securities Studies has conducted any "studies" of the threat to American "security" posed by the KGB or Communist propaganda or subversive activities. The CNSS statement of purpose says that it was founded "to reduce government secrecy, to limit the surveillance of Americans by intelligence agencies, to prohibit surveillance or manipulation of lawful political activity, and to protect the rights of Americans to write and speak on issues affecting the national security." The organization has never attempted to study the degree of surveillance of American citizens or American defense or industrial activities by Communist intelligence agencies. One hundred percent of its studies have been aimed at the CIA, FBI, and other American agencies. It has ignored the well-documented evidence of Communist espionage and surveillance; for example, the interception of American telecommunications traffic and the massive and growing activities in espionage and propaganda in the U.S. by the KGB and other Soviet organs.

## Institute for Policy Studies

This section arrays the published output of the IPS, classified as to whether it is for or against a Communist line. (For further details on the IPS, see Chapter II.)

The following balance sheet is based on the Fall 1979 IPS Catalogue and a supplement for Summer/Fall 1980. These provide the titles and brief descriptions of 80 publications and 14 films. Ten of the films were directed by Saul Landau and were described earlier in this chapter. Out of the remaining 4 films and 80 publications, 68 are found to be closely parallel to the Communist line in their main subject matter and orientation as described in the IPS Catalogue. For example, many advocate unilateral American disarmament, attack the U.S. intelligence community, or analyze the Americans economy from a "class conflict" point of view. The remaining 14 might most charitably be called neutral. Although not necessarily paralleling A Communist line, even these are generally critical of American institutions, including such titles as *Whistle-Blowers' Guide to the Federal Bureaucracy, Industrial Exodus* ("a classic study of strategies for preventing plant closings and run-away shops") and so forth.

This section does not describe all 84 items in the IPS Catalogue, but presents a sampling of typical titles and quotes from the descriptions given in the catalogue. (Emphasis has been added in some of the descriptions.)

DEBITS:

— *The Politics of National Security* by Marcus Raskin. "This historical analysis of the *national security state* traces its evolution from a planning instrument to ensure national stability, *mute class conflicts,* and secure the domestic economy to the basis for overt and covert *imperialism.* The debacle in Indochina, *the genocidal nature of the arms race.... etc.*"

— *The Search for 'Manchurian Candidate': The CIA and Mind Control* by John Marks.

— *The Lawless State: The Crimes of the Intelligence Community* by Halperin, Borosage, Berman, and Marwick.

— *The Counterforce Syndrome* by Robert C. Aldrige. "How 'counterforce' has replace 'deterrence' contrary to what most Americans believe...."

— *Dubious Specter—A Second Look at the "Soviet Threat"* by Fred Kaplan.

— *The Rise and Fall of the "Soviet Threat"* by Alan Wolfe.

— *Resurgent Militarism* by Michael T. Klare. "An analysis of the growing militaristic fervor which is spreading from Washington across the nation...."

— *NATO's Unremarked Demise* by Earl C. Ravenal. "A critique of the Atlantic Alliance.... This study refutes two assumptions

137

of the post WW II era: that the defense of Europe is required for the balance of power, and that 'interdependence' is required for our national security. A drastically changed international system invites American disengagement from Europe."

—*The Economy of Death* by Richard J. Barnet. ". . . . this trenchant analysis of the defense budget exposes how the military-industrial complex manipulates public expenditures to squander vast sums in useless hardware. . . . Social costs of this waste require a program of national conversation to an 'Economy of Life' achieved by citizen action in defiance of this threat."

—*Intervention and Revolution* by Richard J. Barnet. "A classic study of American intervention in developing nations. This lucid work refutes the Cold War tenets of U.S. foreign policy and documents the *history of repressive military intervention.*

—*The Sullivan Principles: Decoding Corporate Camouflage* by Elizabeth Schmidt. "An analysis of the Sullivan Principles, the fair employment code devised by American corporations in South Africa to deflect public criticism of investment in that country." (Actually, this code was not developed by American corporations but by the Rev. Leon H. Sullivan, pastor of the Zion Baptist Church, the largest church in North Philadelphia, and one of the most respected black ministers in the U.S. Sullivan devised these principles as a means of allowing the blacks in South Africa to have the benefits of employment by American corporations without the corporations being parties to encouragement of apartheid.)

—*How the Other Half Dies* by Susan George. "This examination of multinational agribusiness corporations explains that the roots of hunger are not overpopulation, changing climate, or bad weather, but rather control of food by the rich."

—*The Dead Are Not Silent.* Film produced by Studio H & S of Communist East Germany, describes the overthrow of the Allende government in Chile as told by two women—Isabel Letelier and Moy de Toha.

CREDITS:

No publications are listed that could be considered to oppose a Communist line in any respect. In none of the many studies of U.S. defense policies is there any recognition of the danger of the Soviet arms build-up. In fact, many of the books specifically discount this threat. There is no mention of the work of the KGB or Soviet propaganda organs. While there is considerable treatment of American multi-nationals and "monopolies,' there is nothing about the problems of Communist monopolistic practices in such areas as grain purchasing or the setting of shipping rates, which is now causing grave problems for free world shipping.

# XI. Conclusions and Recommendations

While many observers in the U.S. and abroad have been alarmed and mystified by America's loss of will during the past decade, virtually no one has identified Communist propaganda as a principal cause. A notable exception is Andrei Sakharov, the great Russian dissident. In his latest book, *My Country and the World,* he speaks of the loss of will among elites in the West due to "an unrelenting stream of mendacious propaganda aided and abetted by fellow-travelling intellectuals."

The case histories in previous chapters were designed to show the effects of such propaganda in affecting American media and hence public opinion and even government policy. We selected these to illustrate crises in American policy where media treatment of the issues can now be shown to have been based so clearly on *falsehoods* and at the same time *to have fol-*

*lowed so closely the Communist line* that the treatment must have been executed either by Communist
agents or sympathizers or by well-meaning people being manipulated.

Who are the agents behind such bias or manipulation? There is little firm evidence, because of the inhi-
bitions placed in recent years on FBI investigations of
subversion and the dismantling of the Congressional
Internal Security committees in the 1970s. In countries where the security agencies are allowed to conduct investigations, such as Singapore and Malaysia,
they have unearthed large networks of agents influencing media performance and government policy, as
described in Chapter III.

How is the Communist propaganda effort organized? A major portion of the effort is now imple-
mented by Americans working within this country.
Before World War II and up through the early 1960s,
the major portion of the propaganda emanated directly from Communist media. But beginning in the
1960s and increasing part of this was being carried out
by American agents and sympathizers working within
this country. In the case studies of Cambodia, the
North Vietnamese, AID, and the CIA, for example, we
can see that most of the slogans and tactics for stimu-
lating Congressional investigations and recommendations for new legislation, were devised by Americans
in the Far Left Lobby or the media. They were following, knowingly or unknowingly, major objectives laid
down in Moscow (or Peking), but were adding to
them their expertise in how best to influence American opinion.

## Conclusions

So the conclusions of this study can be summarized in just 9 points:

1. The Communists' drive for world domination has been making relentless progress since World War II. In 1945, the Soviet Union controlled 7% of the earth's population. Following the latest takeovers, Communist governments now dominate more than 33%. Americans should be concerned about the survival of the free world if this trend continues, but recent Communist victories have been virtually unopposed.

2. The Communists have been succeeding by subversion and propaganda as much as by military means. Throughout history, from Lenin and his successors, they have regarded propaganda as being as important a weapon as physical force in gaining power.

3. There are more than three million people, "agit-prop cadres," *within the Soviet Union,* engaged full time on propaganda directed *at the Soviet population.*

4. There are more than a half million Communist propaganda agents working around the world outside the Soviet Union, spending more than $3 billion a year on propaganda.

5. The United States is the number one target, "Glavny Vrag," the main enemy.

6. A substantial percent of these half million agents are operating within the United States, at least 4,000 and possibly many more, spending over $240 million annually on propaganda.

7. There are several levels of propaganda agents.

Their activity can be classified from high to low as follows:

—Russian (or other Communist country agents in the U.S.)

—American agents (usually not Party members).

—Opportunists who follow the Communist line for the sake of their careers.

—Idealists being manipulated, often without their knowledge.

8. Many journalists have been following the Communist line. Only a few of these individuals have been identified as Communists, and these are almost all in the older generation. The reason is that American intelligence agencies have been crippled in recent years and the Congressional internal security committees have been dismantled. So there have been no government authorities capable of determining who may be agents. Instead, this study has used two other techniques: a) the Balance Sheet Method, to assess the output of major media personalities and show the degree of Communist influence—summarized in Chapter X, and b) the Cast History Method.

These propaganda activities have been having a devastating effect in undermining America's will power abroad, causing defeats in such areas as Viet Nam and Cambodia; distorting public attitudes towards American institutions like the CIA, the FBI, and the Agency for International Development; and weakening our defense and intelligence efforts.

9. Propaganda is the only area where the Communists are superior to the Free World. In economics, internal morale, human freedoms, scientific development, and weapons (at least until recent years), we surpass them. But if the trends of the past

thirty years persist, the Communists may succeed in taking over the world by subversion and propaganda, backed by their eventual use of force, even though the majority of the people are against them.

## Recommendations

The key to defeating propaganda is to expose it as such. We Americans should do at least the following:

1. Restore the FBI's authorization to investigate subversive activity, reactivate the internal security committees of the Senate the the House of Representatives. As part of their new duties, there should be an investigation of Communist propaganda activities in the U.S.

2. An increase in the valuable work done by private organizations such as the useful studies on the total propaganda picture by the Church League of America, the American Security Council, Accuracy in Media and Information Digest.

3. The results of both private and public investigations should be made public whenever possible.

4. It is not enough to expose falsehood. One must also disseminate the truth. The government's own information agencies (the ICA, Voice of America, Radio Free Europe, etc.) should be strengthened. These organizations should become more vigorous in drawing attention to aggressive Communist behavior around the world and in defending American policies.

5. There is a need for more control of the media.

Perhaps there is enough competition in print media so that no Government control is needed, but the near monopoly of the 3 major TV networks has become so powerful in opinion formation that national survival demands some assurance that they will not be free to disseminate the misinformation and distortions that have occurred in recent years. The Fairness Doctrine was passed to guard against propaganda from the right but has proved to be ineffective against propaganda from the left. A preliminary recommendation for a solution to this problem is to require an ombudsman for each major network (such as exist on some newspapers), but appointed by an independent outside body such as the FCC. This individual would be responsible to see that the Fairness Doctrine is followed and that the networks are employing adequate expert advice on any major issues arising in the news, such as nuclear weapons, intelligence, internal security, defense, and foreign policy, all of which have become much more complex in recent years.

## What Private Citizens Can Do

Some of the most powerful work to counter the Communist propaganda offensive can be done by Americans working as individuals or in citizen groups.

1. Monitor your own local media. Do the popular columnists or broadcast commentators in your area tend to show a heavy tilt towards policies that parallel the Communist line? If so, ask them and editors, news

directors and media owners for explanations. Broadcasting stations must keep your letters on file for review at license renewal time: this is one of the most powerful tools we citizens have for controlling the electronic media.

2. Monitor the national organization of your church or temple. If the organization is active politically and you see a title towards the pro-Communist side, demand an explanation and review its contribution policies.

3. Monitor the votes and speeches of your Congressman and Senator. If you disagree, write. If you fail to get a satisfactory explanation, work for an opposing candidate.

4. Monitor any Congressman and Senators from your state on the Foreign Affairs, Intelligence, Justice, or Armed Services Committees. If their policies don't tend to strengthen the U.S., write.

5. Keep abreast of major decisions before Congress and the Administration. Write to your Senator and Congressman to support the policies that strengthen the U.S.

6. Join citizens' organizations active in working for a stronger America (labor unions, veterans groups, etc.)

7. If you are in a profession, consider joining or forming a professional organization to offset pro-Communist activities.

8. Everything you do as a private individual in travelling or doing business abroad has some effect on America's image and the impression of the U.S. as a free enterprise democracy. You and your business or

trade association may be able to cooperate in promoting America's cause in foreign countries.

9. It is even possible for you to have a direct influence behind the Iron Curtain, by assisting those in Communist countries who are attempting to worship as they please. Several organizations in the U.S. and Europe, such as the Christian Anti-Communist Crusade and the Eastern European Bible Mission, are carrying on campaigns to send bibles into Communist countries and in other ways help believers there worship as they see fit.

This is only a bare outline of recommendations for countering the Communists propaganda campaign. Such propaganda is the one superior weapon the Communists wield in their offensive against the Free World. One reason it is so powerful is that it is so little known. If we can unmask the propaganda offensive, if we can overcome this one advantage the Communist have over the free world, we can arrest the continual threat, stave off defeat, and turn it into a victory—and we can do it without a nuclear war.

# THE AIM REPORT

Americans spend billions of dollars for information. Unfortunately, much of it is misinformation and disinformation.

Disinformation works because few people realize they are being disinformed.

Accuracy in Media is a unique organization which exposes and seeks corrections of serious errors, distortions and omissions by the major news media.

Twice a month it publishes the AIM Report, which reveals with carefully documented facts the serious sins of CBS, NBC, ABC, *The New York Times, The Washington Post* and others.

You can discover how the media misinforms and disinforms millions of Americans for as little as $15 a year. That is the cost of membership in AIM, which entitles you to get 24 fact-filled issues of the AIM Report.

In addition, your membership in AIM is tax-deductible, as are larger donations to AIM. Your membership and your donations help support AIM's vigorous efforts to set the record straight in a wide variety of ways. These include:

- A weekly syndicated newspaper column carried by 100 newspapers.
- A daily radio commentary aired by 80 radio stations
- A speakers' bureau that provides outstanding speakers free of charge to groups throughout the country
- Sending hundreds of letters to editors, giving radio and TV interviews
- Attending shareholder meetings of the media giants to call the management to account for their errors and distortions

*Be informed! Join AIM! Read the AIM Report!*

*TO:* **AIM,** PO Box 2890, Washington, D.C. 20005

☐ Enclosed is $ _____ for my membership in AIM. ($15 minimum, $30 to get the AIM Report by faster first class mail, $100 and up for patrons.)

Name _____

Address _____

City, State, Zip _____